DOUBLE OR QUIT

DOUBLE OR QUIT

Joyce Stranger

Michael Joseph
LONDON

First published in Great Britain by
Michael Joseph Ltd
27 Wrights Lane,
London W8 5TZ
1987

Photographs by Seán Hagerty

British Library Cataloguing in Publication Data
Stranger, Joyce
    Double or quit.
    I. Title
    828'.91408   PR6069.T48
    ISBN 0–7181–2959–8

Typeset in Bembo at The Spartan Press Ltd,
Lymington, Hants
Printed and bound in Great Britain by Billings and Sons, Worcester

Dedicated to my sister June and her husband, Jerrold;
to my sister Sheila, and to my brother David and his
wife Helen,
who all wonder why on earth their sister has dogs!
So, sometimes, do I.
Though very rarely.

Illustrations

Chapter One

There is nothing quite like starting with a new dog. It is a new adventure; a new individual to learn about, and a great deal of learning to be done. I had just bought another dog and couldn't wait to bring him home. He was a large German Shepherd, a handsome fellow, black and gold, with a beautiful head, an affectionate manner, and he was, we thought, about two years old, or just under.

I had always said I would never take on an adult dog, a dog that someone else had already shaped, a dog that might have bad habits, and above all, I wouldn't take on a male German Shepherd, as they are powerful dogs, and if they do have bad habits, they are strong-minded animals and may not be easy to re-teach.

The best of making one's own rules is that they can be broken. I met Josse; I fell for him; and I bought him. I surely had enough dog experience to take him on.

I teach in dog club, and fully half our dogs are dogs with second, third or fourth homes. I knew there would be initial problems, many of them. I knew it would be fully a year before the dog became really mine, if he did attach. Some never do, and remain unrewarding, unaffectionate animals, who have been brought up without human companionship and neither want it nor need it.

In the past fifteen years I have had three dogs. My first was Janus, my Golden Retriever, who was deaf, and who died when he was thirteen. He was a wonderful dog, a clown of a dog, with a sense of humour mostly dedicated to making me look a fool. My second in those years was Puma, my first German Shepherd, who had lead poisoning when young, and who died of the belated effects of that when she was nine years old.

Then there was Chita, my second German Shepherd who

was a demon puppy, and who had to be civilised. Training her brought me into contact with people who trained their dogs to police dog standard, and taught me a great deal about dogs.

Chita has one problem. She is full of energy. She adores life, is immensely curious, and her small enquiring nose manages to get her into mischief, through an inability to control her desire to find out what lies over the hill, or behind the hedge, or under the rug.

I had to learn to curb that enthusiasm and channel it, so that she did no harm to herself or to others. Now, at nearly nine years old, she was tremendous fun, but she lacked company, and without Janus, who had died recently, was becoming depressed. I wanted another dog too, but not a puppy. An adult dog, which would play with Chita, and when she went, as go she must in the fullness of time, I would have a dog still at my side.

There was a great deal to do before I brought my new dog home. Eric Roberts, who had sold him to me, was sure he was a dog which would be happier in a kennel than indoors. The dog had been the sole companion of a very elderly man for a year. His owner then died, and the dog went to one son for a week, to a second son for a week and then to the RSPCA. He was then bought to train for protection work but he didn't stand up to the intensive discipline, and was sold on.

He had been kennelled for over six months. He was no longer a house dog, if he ever had been.

We built him a kennel and run. I went over once a week to spend the day with the dog, to let him run with Chita, and to get him used to me and my car. He had changed hands so often in a mere six months that another change was sure to be difficult for him. At least he would know me and Chita and my car before we started out on the long journey home. It would, so far as I knew, be the longest journey he had ever made.

Eric meanwhile was teaching him to come when called, to understand the meaning of 'no', to walk on the lead properly, and generally to behave himself. He rang during that three weeks to say that the dog was much livelier than he had realised, and that he wondered if he was the right dog for me.

But I had set my heart on Josse, partly because he was named with the name of the dog in a novel, *Josse*, I had written some years before.

At last the day came and I went to collect my new dog. He came out of the kennel and ran to Eric, who had been his owner for the past nine weeks. Eric's kennels are a staging post for many dogs, too good to put down, unwanted by their owners for one reason or another, and for sale. Some stay there for many months until the right owner is found.

Dogs adore Eric, which I suspect makes it hard for them to re-attach to a new owner. He has a way with them that is shared by few other people. Josse bounded up to him when the kennel girl brought the dog out, though she then had to hand the lead to me. But Josse didn't see why I should hold him. He wanted a familiar person – not someone he barely knew.

I left Chita in the car and walked my new dog up into the country park. He came biddably, but he wasn't interested in me. He was interested in the smell of sheep and rabbit, and was happy enough to be free from the confines of the kennel. He was used to being walked by three different kennel girls, or by Eric, or by Eric's new wife, Liz. As far as Josse was concerned, I was just another person, of no significance to him at all. He pulled on the lead, and I checked him. He didn't intend to be checked and we had an argument, which did end with me winning.

He was no more powerful than Chita, who although she is small for her breed, is very strong indeed. He was much bigger. His head was on a level with my thigh, and he was longer than she.

He had an air about him that I liked, and I hoped very much that he would settle with us, and be as successful as my past three dogs. There was a great deal that was unknown about him. He would, in a way, be a living detective story which I had to unravel, as I would have to find out what were his bad points and what were his good points, and would have to work to make him live under my rules. He had known six different sets of rules already. His behaviour generally would tell me a great deal about his past, and what he had been allowed to do.

3

I knew how Eric had kept him and I knew what he had taught the dog. I knew nothing about his past before that. Training to walk at heel is all very well but it doesn't stop a dog chasing cats if he has been allowed to get away with that.

Hopefully he was young enough to re-train. For all I knew he could be a fighter, or he could be a villain. He had little chance to misbehave when kept in kennels and exercised briefly, alone, in an isolated place, three times a day, and trained, again without any distractions, in a field, once or twice a day.

I hoped to give him much more freedom, and have him, like Chita, as my daily companion. After our walk I went into the training field. Josse behaved very well on the lead, walking close at heel, apparently enjoying himself. His tail waved and he bounced several times at my hand. Highly delighted, I took him off the lead.

'Josse, heel.'

Josse streaked down the field and back to his kennel. The door was shut, cleaned ready for a new occupant, who was to move in as soon as Josse had gone. It was coming that afternoon, a dog that nobody wanted, because there had been a divorce in the family. Another young German Shepherd, this time a bitch. Josse tried to paw the kennel door open, but it was bolted. He came away disconsolately. He had no home at all.

I found him standing by my car. He had been inside it three times already, and it was better than being trained off the lead. I put him in with Chita, and went to have lunch.

After lunch both dogs came out of the car and ran together. At least, that was my idea – but they had different ideas. Josse commuted between the car and his kennel, and then, adventuring down the long field, found the scent left by a bitch in season, and happily followed that. She had been exercised on the field that morning. Her presence meant that most of the male dogs howled in unison, triggered by the scent on the air. It was a noisy background.

Presently the two dogs did meet, sniffed one another, and ran down the field together. Chita is a chunky little bitch, solid and very well muscled. Josse, much younger, taller by several inches, looked thin beside her, all head and no body.

4

Their markings were very similar and both had gleaming coats. This is due to the type of food they receive. Josse, I discovered, was fed the same way as Chita, so that was no problem. I would not have to buy different foods, or try to change him over. Often dog foods are regional and what is available in one part of the country can't be found in another.

He came to me happily enough so long as Eric wasn't there. If Eric was there, I could whistle till next week. The dog was not going to change loyalties. He would work with me on the lead, while Eric exercised his own dogs, but off the lead, he bolted again, this time to my car, having apparently decided the kennel was no longer his. Its new occupant was already inside, and he had gone back just once more, and been startled to find his home of the past nine weeks occupied. He appeared to realise the kennel was no longer his, and afterwards, when panic overtook him, he went to my car. He never tried to get into that kennel again.

I separated the two dogs for the journey to Anglesey. There were over one hundred and twenty miles to drive, and I did not want to risk a fight. I had no idea how they would settle together. Chita came in front with me, lying on the passenger seat, a position she was used to. Josse went behind the dog guard.

Josse travelled extremely well. I was afraid he might be carsick, but he was obviously used to travelling. He lay quietly, or sat, watching the traffic. He was curious and alert, but unresponsive to me. He watched me, weighing me up. His tail didn't wag at all. He had no choice but to be with me, but he didn't have to be enthusiastic about it.

When we reached home I let him explore at the end of a twenty-foot line. There was a big field to investigate and there were dozens of interesting smells, especially where birds had landed and hunted for insects in the grass – Josse was fascinated by these areas. We have pheasants and partridges, as well as magpies galore. I didn't learn till much later that birds were to play an important part in our lives together.

He snuffled under the back door. Inside the house there was Chia, our Siamese cat. She took one horrified look through the window, at this strange, huge dog come to stay, and vanished.

Eric may have taught him to come when called – to Eric. He had no intention of coming to me, and it was not until I produced a bowl of food that he condescended to leave his own affairs and join me. From then on, exercise – even at home – would have to be on the long line. I had to teach him that what I said was as important as what Eric said.

I took him to his kennel. It smelt all wrong. No dog had been inside it. Everything was new. I sat on Josse's bed, with Chita on one side and Josse on the other, and stroked him. He lay with his head on my knee, his eyes staring into the distance. He was a forlorn dog, a bewildered dog, and though he appeared to respond, and seemed relatively unstressed, he was very stressed, but just didn't show it.

I took Chita in and fed her while Josse ate his food. He was shut in the run, and didn't like it. He wanted to be with me, as I was better than no one. But Eric had been insistent that I was to keep him in the kennel, and not bring him into the house at first, and Eric was the expert. Josse bolted his food, and was instantly sick. It was the only obvious sign he gave of being upset by his change of owner.

'He'll howl at first,' Eric had said. 'Dogs always do when they first come to a new home.' I knew that. I was often at Callanway, where Eric lives, when a new dog came in, and the next twenty-four hours were apt to be noisy, the dog alternately barking and howling, wanting its owner and its familiar surroundings. After that, they usually settled. Some dogs settle easily. It all depends on the dog.

They never howled if they came back a second time. This was now familiar.

Josse howled and yipped until 2 am; I lay listening and worrying. Suppose he never settled? Suppose I had to take him back?

I thought of all our club rescue dogs. I knew what the owners went through, some for months on end. It isn't easy for a dog to change homes. Josse had changed so often that this might be the final cracking point, as he had already cracked up under training. He was a sensitive dog.

6

He was far more sensitive than Chita, who if she banged into something said the canine equivalent of 'oh blow', barked and carried on with whatever she had been doing. Josse had run down the drive that first evening and bumped into my car, and though he hadn't really hurt himself, he had come for comfort and spent about five minutes feeling sorry for his poor hurt side. Chita had watched in amazement.

That sensitivity might well prove to be detrimental to this last change of home. I hoped my neighbours couldn't hear the dog. I hoped the two dogs would get on. I hoped that Chia would settle down and at least tolerate him, but that might have been asking a lot at fourteen years old. She was a very elderly cat.

She must have been disturbed by the noise too as she began her favourite game. The mysterious clickings in the night had puzzled us for a long time, until one day I saw Chia sitting on the bathroom shelf, engrossed in playing catch with the wooden acorn switch on the light cord.

Luckily she can't pull it down. Instead she bats it at the wall, and when she has insomnia the clicks become raps. She had insomnia that night, and her clicks and raps added to Josse's wails.

'Don't go to him,' Eric had said.

All the same I was very glad when morning came, and got up at five thirty to investigate, leaving Chita, indignant, in her polythene dogproof bed, which was not Chita-proof, as it has frayed edges where she chewed it as a pup.

I went out into a sunlit dawn. It was cold, as it was a late spring, and May brought frosts. But there had been no frost that night. I left footmarks in the dew, and went, with Josse's long line, over to his kennel. He couldn't be left free as he might run off. It was obvious from his night noises that he didn't think much of his new home.

Had I done wrong in buying him, and trying to re-home him? Perhaps he would have been better left with Eric, but then he would have gone elsewhere and they too would have had problems.

What had I done by bringing this dog home?

I was soon to find out. As ever, nothing turned out the way any of us had expected.

Not even Eric, who had summed Josse up as an easy dog.

He wrote later that we were to see a very different side of Josse in the months to come.

Chapter Two

Josse was out of his kennel, and that mystified me. The kennel door had been bolted and the run was padlocked, as dogs have been known to be stolen and we all make sure our dogs are secure when left for the night. German Shepherds have a high priority as they make guard dogs, and can be sold abroad.

He was leaping up, trying to jump over the weldmesh. As that was six feet high, and had a ridge at the top which leaned inwards to prevent just that, he was not having much success. The left-hand lower boards of the kennel, which were beside the central door, were piled in a neat heap beside him.

He had no breath left for crying. His noise was odd, a very distinctive puppy yip, which sounded most peculiar coming from such a big dog.

He had plainly had as bad a night as I had. He was warm, very warm, when I went inside the run. Today, since I had no competition, and was the only person in his world, he greeted me. He greeted me with such fervour that I was pinned against the mesh, with his paws on my shoulder, and his tongue devouring me.

I put him on the long line and took him outside. He behaved for a few minutes like a salmon on a line, racing all over the place, pulling to get away from me. I talked to him, gently and softly. I knelt and held out my arms, and he came into them. After a few minutes of stroking him, and talking quietly, the worry died out of his eyes. That worried look, which was to last for months, gave him a haunted expression. Everything was strange to him, and he was not at all sure what was going to happen. He didn't trust me, not one little bit.

I had a suspicion that he thought I was yet another staging post, and that dogs changed homes every few weeks. His experience with Eric had not been continuous, as Eric had married while Josse was there, and Josse, together with Eric's own dogs, had gone to a friend's kennels for a week. Yet another new place, and yet more new people. Maybe he thought he would pass on again and again, never knowing security, neither having the benefit of a set routine, nor of one or two permanent people in his life. That security had gone for him when his owner died.

I found myself wondering more and more about that first owner, and whether he had known he was leaving his dog, and had died unhappy because of that. I knew I would worry terribly in similar circumstances, unless death came suddenly. It soon transpired in the weeks to come that Josse had been a very well-loved pet, used to a great deal of attention, and had been given a certain amount of indoor training, although he appeared to have had no training – apart from that Eric had given him – as regards going out and about and meeting people and dogs.

But on that first day there were more immediate things to bother about. Josse had refused to empty himself the night before, and now he was bursting. I was afraid he might harm himself by hanging on like that. When I spoke to Eric, I discovered that it is very usual for dogs not to empty themselves until they are used to a place, and can relax. There is nothing one can do about it except wait for the inevitable, and hope it happens sooner rather than later.

I always teach my dogs to empty on command. Chita, let out late at night, would perform at once and come in for her last biscuit. Josse, on his first night, kept me walking round and round the garden, for nearly two hours, until I had to give up from sheer exhaustion, as it was past midnight, and put him back in his run, where he howled and yipped for me to come back.

That puppy yip, coupled with the fact that he did not cock his leg, but still squatted like an immature dog, made me wonder if he were younger than we thought. There is no way of knowing. His age will always be a guess. When I wrote to the Kennel Club to register him for Working Trials (all working dogs must be registered with them, crossbreeds as well as the pedigrees, if they are to be shown), they set his birthday on 1 January 1984. Obviously dogs who have to be described as 'All Further Details Unknown' are like race-horses, and start on the first day of the year in which they were probably born.

Once he was comfortable Josse did not want to wander. He wanted to lean against me. He had been alone in a strange place all night and he needed contact. I changed the long line for his short lead and he came willingly. I took him down our lane and out into the street, and he walked beside me, a calm dog, behaving immaculately. I was delighted with him.

Till he saw a cat.

Up went his ears, his eyes brightened, and he lunged forward, unbalancing me completely. The cat, being wise, took off at speed and vanished over a wall, and I recovered myself, realising I had yet another hazard to watch, and some training to put in. That was not going to be easy. I have known dogs that killed cats. Josse was evidently not catproof, though he had been proof against the cat that haunted Eric's kennels. That however was a different cat and a different situation.

He had not yet met Chia, and I wondered just how to manage that particular confrontation, as Chia loathes, not only strange dogs, but also strange people. Very few of our visitors are privileged by her presence. She retreats to my wardrobe, only appearing for her last meal, late at night, when the intruders have either gone home, or are safely in bed in our spare room.

I realised from Josse's attitude that the introduction would be far from easy.

Dogs unfortunately don't learn as we do. Josse had learned that he shouldn't chase cats at Callanway; he hadn't learned that he shouldn't chase cats in our village street. Nor had he lived in close proximity to a cat, as the cat that visited the kennels belonged next door.

We reached home at 6.30 am and I put him back in his run and fetched Chita so that she could have a little time to herself. We played her quoit game, which she loved. She would fetch that quoit endlessly, and my arm tired long before she did.

I gave Josse some biscuits to eat. He was sitting in the run, watching us. I fussed him, and went in for my own breakfast and Chita followed me. I had a suspicion that this kennelling business was not going to work. I didn't like leaving one dog outside while the other came in. Also Kenneth had gone away, and I couldn't repair the kennel. There was no point in putting Josse in a kennel with a large hole in it at night. I didn't know where he was going to sleep.

I took him briefly indoors and while I was on the phone, he flooded the carpet. Indoors would have to be delayed, as I needed to be free to watch him. I took him outside again and put him in my car. He was used to that now, and as he was kennel-clean he was likely to be car-clean too. Chita was used to being with me while I worked or went about the various household chores, and she settled. She was puzzled by the newcomer, and though prepared to tolerate him, she was jealous, and sometimes, when I went out to him in the weeks that followed, she sat indoors and howled, a long, forlorn wolfhowl.

It wasn't possible to train the two of them together, as one would interfere while I worked with the other. Josse needed a great deal more time spending with him than Chita, who was now so easy and rarely made a mistake.

I wanted Josse vetted, and he needed injections, so our next visit was for that. My dogs have always liked visiting the vet, and tolerated whatever is done to them. Most dogs, as they grow older, realise they go when something is wrong, and that the visit is succeeded by feeling better.

Josse came out of the car at the vet's, and then tried to get back in again. He was on the lead, and we were going into a house, and I was sure he thought he was going to be left here. If he were in the car, he knew he couldn't be left behind. It was very difficult indeed to persuade him to come in with me.

As we came in through the waiting-room door the vet's assistant came out of the operating theatre, moving fast, dressed in a long green coat and his surgeon's cap. Josse launched himself at Steve, snarling and barking, a dog transformed. Steve leaped back and I got Josse under control and tried to pacify him. Steve vanished and we sat, waiting. I had asked for an appointment, rather than risk a crowded waiting-room at surgery time, as this dog was a completely unknown quantity.

Barbara, the nurse, experienced in her dealings with all types of dogs over long years, came out armed with a supply of broken biscuits from the morning-coffee tin. Steve came back, this time without his cap and gown, and, crouching down to make himself small, held out the biscuits. Josse was wary, but he took them and allowed Steve to stroke him.

We had a while to wait, as Ellis, the senior vet, who was on surgery duty, was not yet ready for us. All went well until Polly, the vet's marmalade cat, came out of the office. Polly is sure she is a dog, and equally sure all dogs must like her. She was used to rubbing herself against Janus and Puma, and to rubbing noses with Chita. She came forward towards Josse, and Josse leaped.

Polly was up on the reception counter in an instant, scattering papers and swearing, while I held on to my dog. It was a relief to go into the surgery, though Josse greeted Ellis with a harsh growl. I shook the dog. 'No.'

'Are you keeping him?' asked my vet, who, I suspect, was dubious, and not all happy about this latest patient. I assured him I was and then for some reason had a sudden feeling that the trouble was not the two men, but the coats they were wearing. When I suggested this Ellis took his off and Josse visibly relaxed, though he did growl softly when the needle went in.

Later that day, when shopping, I took Josse to the bank and then to the butcher. Josse behaved beautifully in the bank, but the butcher and his white coat provoked another long loud growl. A few days later in our village street we met the baker, also in a white coat. Josse snarled at once, and the rumbling growl was even more pronounced. My baker, however, is used to dogs, and instead of taking off his coat, he began to talk to Josse.

'What a fuss. What's all that about then? You silly dog.'

After a few minutes the dog relaxed and allowed the man to pet him.

We repeated that visit a number of times, as well as going to the vet and going in with Josse when I took newspapers for the hospital cages, which I did about once a week. He came in with far less protest after a few weeks, but for months we raced back to the car, as Josse was determined to get in there fast. The car meant he was coming back with me, not being left behind. We all hoped he would not need any residential treatment in his first few months with us.

Gradually, the vet became an acceptable part of Josse's life too. Chita, who adores men, and particularly Ellis, regards vet-going as a treat, and can't wait to get in. I have to watch that her greeting is not too enthusiastic as one day Ellis had opened his arms and said, 'How's my girl?' and as he had bent to stroke her Chita had leaped up and almost broke his nose. We weren't very popular. She can't be greeted with too much fervour, as it still triggers her to major excitement, in spite of her matronly years.

Last time we visited, Josse met three men in white coats, all in one room, and sat and gave them his paw. He relaxed while I talked to them. But it had taken more than a year to achieve that, and we had to visit regularly, and make sure he knew that this place was safe, and that he would never be left behind there. We hoped that that would not be necessary until long after the dog had settled and realised that his home was now with us for good. Now he can walk to the car too, not drag me faster than I can move, in his desperate desire to reach it.

That desire did not only apply when we visited the vet's. It applied whenever he left the car. After a few minutes away, he had to get back, had to make sure he was safe, had to be certain he was coming home with me and not going to be handed over to the next person who approached us, or be left in a strange shop or house, while I vanished never to return.

I was going over to Eric's once a week, to train both dogs: Chita with other would-be working triallers, Josse in a group, to get him used to other dogs. The first few minutes were always bad, as he lunged and barked at any dog that moved. We had been unlucky on our first walk in the local park, as a black Labrador, off-lead, had attacked Josse, who was on-lead. I was in danger of being bitten, and dropped the lead. Josse fought back, the other dog's owners managed to call it off, and Josse came back to me, and immediately we bolted for the car.

He will retaliate if attacked, but he hates fighting, and if he can will run behind me. His aggression wasn't boldness, but fear. However, he had to learn not to retaliate or I would have a dog I couldn't take anywhere. The learning was wearisome. Check, no, relax the check and praise so long as he was quiet again. Never praise when he was barking or growling as he would think I was approving the bad behaviour. My friend Sheila, from Chesterfield, who also came to Eric's classes, was having the same problem with her young German Shepherd Dog, Coda, and hers was not a re-homed dog.

The first few minutes of any lesson were extremely difficult, with both Sheila and I having to check our big powerful youngsters over and over again until they realised we were not going to allow them to react to each other or to other dogs. Josse was particularly averse to black Labradors after the attack in the park and there was one in the class.

After our third lesson Eric watched us race for the car, Josse almost pulling me over in his desire to get there – and get there fast – and make sure he was coming home, and not being left behind again. It was impossible to check him. All I could do was hang on. He was so determined.

Eric watched us, and took the dog from me. He tried to make Josse sit, but Josse had only one goal in mind – the car. After a five-minute battle I was handed my dog with the comment, 'You have got a problem.'

It was a problem that was to remain for months. We approached the car, and I sat the dog. I sat him before I opened the door. I made him wait to get in. This was fine in places he knew. But take him to a strange place and panic set in.

'Must reach the car. Must reach the car.' There was nothing else in Josse's mind. He was deaf to all commands; he didn't notice the lead check; he didn't, when set on that particular course of action, notice other people or other dogs. He put his head down, pulled into his collar, and went.

One morning, about a month after I brought Josse home, I promised a club member a lesson. She arrived early with her very unruly but delightful Collie, who was as full of energy as

Josse was. I was teaching Josse in the park, and asked her to wait while I put him in the car. He tried to take off, far faster than I could walk.

I checked him, walked in the opposite direction, saying 'no' very firmly, and tried again. And again. And again. I was not going to go back at his pace. If the habit wasn't broken it would be with us for the rest of his life. It was half an hour before I managed to get him back at a fairly reasonable walk, sit him, open the door, keep him sitting, and then let him in. I wondered if he would ever learn.

I started Sam's lesson, and apologised to his owner.

'That did me more good than the lesson,' she said. 'I would have given up. You didn't. I see now what I'm doing wrong with Sam. I'm letting him win.' A month later she came into class beaming, her once unmanageable dog beside her.

'Can I swank?' she asked.

As everyone had seen the struggle she had with Sam and the way he played her up, I grinned and said, 'of course'. She removed Sam's lead, and walked twice round the hall, the dog close at heel, watching her, and ignoring everything else. It was an incredible performance, after the weeks of battle the two had had.

'How did you do that?' I asked.

'I realised that even *you* can't have a dog behave all the time, or every time, and that it wasn't me being incompetent. It was me not trying hard enough, and giving up and letting the dog have his own way. He now knows who is boss – and he isn't.'

I might be struggling with Josse, suffering from the dog's past, but having him was paying bonuses, as Chita is so well behaved people don't realise that she too, in her early days, gave me major problems. Seeing me having to work to gain mastery, people stop assuming I can do it, and that they can't, and their attitude to their own capabilities changes.

Those first weeks were memorable, in that in spite of the trips over to Eric one thing after another triggered Josse to growling, snarling, barking and lunging: men who came too near to me; other dogs, especially if they were off-lead and ran at him, barking, as so many did; anyone who came to the house.

16

As the kennel needed more repair than I had realised, Josse slept in my car. There, he felt safe. and made no noise at all. He began to come indoors, and never made a mistake in cleanliness again. That one scolding had been enough.

He even managed to tell me if he felt sick, so that he could go outside. Both Puma and Chita did that too though Janus had never managed to. Also Josse watched Chita, and discovered that when I said certain words, she emptied herself, and he followed suit. Eric was right in that the dog was eminently teachable. Within four days I had two dogs that would go out, perform, and come back to me when called, and Josse was coming to me when I called, almost every time. I could let him off-lead, and so long as I didn't try and train him, he was happy.

Once he began to want me, and to realise I was to be a major part of his life, and not yet another transient part, another problem showed. He could not bear me out of sight, – anywhere. In the house, he yipped; in the kennel, he yipped; he yipped if I only went round a corner, or, indoors, into another room. If I left him in the car and walked Chita, as I had to do, he savaged the car.

He made major inroads in the upholstery and as it was only six months old that was tiresome. I had a large piece of multi-ply put against the dog guard and that confined the damage to the part he slept in. Oddly, he was never destructive at night.

The garage owner, from whom I had bought the car, just laughed. They had cars come in that had been stripped by dogs, had had the handbrake and the steering wheel chewed, had had the roof lining torn off. It was a known hazard. One police dog, taken in a car instead of a van after the van broke down, spent the journey quietly demolishing the rear seat he was lying on, much to his handler's dismay. Another took off all the buttons of a uniform coat, but did no other damage.

Chita, left in the car while I trained Josse, decided to howl like a small wolf whenever she was left. She had never done it with Janus. It was tiresome.

I could bear the noise, but didn't like it when other people were about, so tried to walk both dogs together. Chita, who had walked happily with Janus when he was alive, had forgotten how to be part of a team, and resented having to share me. All went moderately well till the day Josse saw a squirrel behind us. He twisted me round and tried to take off, while Chita pulled in the opposite direction. It was remarkably painful.

Chita is used to squirrels, as well as pheasants, partridges, hens, geese and cats, and knew she mustn't chase. There are always squirrels in the park and since it isn't possible to train one dog while holding two, the dogs would have to be walked separately until we had sorted that problem as well. Unfortunately squirrels are unpredictable and don't always oblige by appearing.

When they did Josse had a check on the lead, a sharp 'no', and was made to sit, none of which happened easily. Dogs don't train overnight, and new situations mean a constant rethinking about the way the dog is handled.

Chapter Three

One of the biggest problems I found with a new dog, and one I had forgotten, though I had met it with all my dogs before, was the number of well-meaning people giving advice. It was often good advice, applied to their own dogs. But all dogs being different, it wasn't any use for Josse. Eric was my biggest help as he had known the dog for nine weeks, had worked with him, and had, I discovered, also found that off-lead Josse bolted back to his kennel. On-lead, he had no choice but to work as commanded.

'Give him bags of praise and wrestle with him,' one dog owner advised. We knew that that advice was right for many dogs, but totally wrong for Josse, who has a low threshold of excitement. Bags of praise for Josse resulted in a demented dog leaping up at my face, pushing me flat on my back, yapping and jumping. 'Aren't I clever? Aren't I clever? Aren't I clever?' Chita can take more praise than that but neither can take as much as Megan, the two-year-old black Labrador, who joins us for Sunday ringwork. Megan is a rather sleepy bitch. I can race with her, laughing at her, making her react to far more physical play and verbal encouragement than I can use with either of my own two dogs.

Put Chita and Josse on a downstay, and both are alert, eager, ready to react to any distraction and needing constant reminding and retraining. Megan shines at that. She just goes to sleep!

There was so much to learn about this dog. Eric wanted me to persist with the kennel. He felt certain Josse was an outdoor dog, but I became sure the dog had been kept in the house with his owner for the first months of his life. He began to come in, at first only for short periods. Indoors Josse had his own ways. If I picked up a pan, preparatory to cooking, the dog immediately took himself to a corner and curled up, where he could watch but was never in the way. He didn't need telling. He knew he had to be quiet and lie out of danger. He has a genius for being unobtrusive and can vanish, tucking himself behind a chair, but very watchful, so that if Chita finds a crumb on the floor, he is at once beside her, looking to see if there is another.

Chita invariably follows me out to the kitchen and sits hopefully till told to go to her bed. She is always looking, in case food falls to the ground.

At home, in the next few weeks, as Josse became less stressed, it was also evident that he was an eminently sensible dog. If I picked up my car keys, Chita would fly to the front door, screaming. 'We're going out. We're going out. We're going out.' Josse sat and watched. Was I going to pick my purse up too, or was I merely putting the keys on the shelf where they belonged, having left them on the table?

If I picked up the purse, he realised we were going out, and he joined Chita at the door. He stood there quietly, knowing it would be opened. She appeared certain that she had to make me open it, and always had to be commanded to sit, be quiet, and wait. He would sit, knowing that was the rule. If the keys were put on to the shelf he lay down again. 'Staying in after all.' I had to persuade Chita to leave the front door, as we weren't going out at all. He seemed to know we had already been out and rarely went out twice, while Chita hoped against hope that every time I picked up my car keys we would be driving off. This is still a daily occurrence. Chita can't bear to be kept waiting, and will do a moving sitstay, inching forward all the time.

When the dogs had to get in the car in the garage Chita had problems, while Josse worked out what to do. The doors open in such a way that the dogs need to go to the back of the garage, turn round, and come back again to jump in, otherwise the door blocks them. Josse discovered after one false attempt just what was needed, and did it immediately. Next time he made sure he was in the right position. But Chita has had, for all of her life, to be shown again and again. She simply can't remember, and faced with the door in her way, panics, and rushes round the garage saying she can't get in.

I have to call her, sit her, stroke her, calm her, reassure her, then physically take her to the back of the garage, turn her round, and position her for the jump inside. Josse runs to the back of the garage, twists, as there isn't much room, and puts himself into the right position without any fuss whatever.

In his early days I had trouble with the three basic commands. 'Heel' is easy, as a snatch on the lead tells the dog what he is about to do. That is a signal. And he obeyed 'no' and 'come', almost every time.

But 'sit', 'stand' and 'down' were impossible. I couldn't understand why he didn't obey until one day I tried to imitate Eric's voice. The dog had been owned by six men. I was the first woman in his life. That gruff 'down' got results, but I couldn't reproduce it as I wanted. It was far too difficult to get the tone right every time. It was the tone, not the word, that triggered him.

The dogs always had biscuits, little ones, after their meal. They had to sit for them. Josse soon learned he didn't get a biscuit till be obeyed the word 'sit', and rapidly learned that lesson once it was associated with something he wanted.

I decided that, although Eric is against titbits, so many people I know use them, even when they are training for top competition, that I would too. Within a week Josse knew he had a food reward if he went down, sat or stood for me. Within a fortnight, he would do it without the food.

At home he became the easy dog that Eric had known, so long as he didn't get Chia's scent. Chia panicked if they met, and bolted. If she had only stood her ground I could have cured him and made him accept her. I tried holding her, but was so badly scratched that that had to be discarded as a method of training. I tried walking with her on my shoulder and Josse at heel, in the hall, but she would jump off to the highest point available, and swear at him. In the end they were kept separated and we took care they didn't meet. It was going to be a long time before Josse could go through into Chia's part of the house and not rush at her.

Now, just over a year later, he can meet her, and she will stand still, and let him nose her. If she runs, he chases, but he responds at once to a sharp 'no'. He is young, lively, and a born chaser, and that has had to have major work. It is useless trying to train a dog for competition until he is steady and obeys commands, and can be relied on not to attack other dogs, or give chase to running stock or game. He needs, too, to be safe when out, and even when in our garden, as people come through the gate.

When there were no distractions he was a different animal. He was obviously used to being cuddled and we would get his front legs and the top of his body in our laps, while he moaned with pleasure, and half closed his eyes. Chita, less demonstrative, rapidly became certain she ought to do the same thing, and though she had never asked for petting, and was apt to walk away if offered it, she now made sure she had her share. Strangely, she had never come to be fussed when Janus came for petting, which he often did. But Janus was Chita's pack leader. Josse is not.

This was one area I had to watch, as whichever dog was first at my side pushed the other away, and they were twice on the verge of fighting.

Josse was sitting looking at me thoughtfully one day and I decided to teach him to give me his paw. I tapped his leg, said 'paw', and the next moment received it full in my face, with a tremendous gesture and a look of utter delight. I said it again and was given it with the same gusto. 'Great, I know that. I was taught that, long ago.' He stood up and did a little dance on the spot which was very funny and then gave me his paw again without being asked. He spent the rest of that evening offering it to me, always with that expression of terrific achievement, and it felt as if some barrier had been lifted between us.

Within ten weeks of his arrival the kennel was being used as a store for the club agility apparatus and Josse had his own bed beside Chita's. It saved a great deal of time as I did not have to change bedding daily, or sweep out leaves from the run, and with the dog indoors, he could have the same routine as Chita, could go out at the same times, and could tell me when he needed to go out. I had to make sure that I let him out every hour or so when he was kennelled, and as the kennel was some way from the house, this was also time-consuming. It was horrible if it was wet, and winter would have defeated me, as it is no fun going out in ice and snow and gusty gales to put the dog to bed. I didn't like putting him to bed wet, either. Towels made little difference if there had been a real downpour.

His morning greeting to me, once he was in the house, was odd. He was always sitting at the door when I came down. He would hide his head under my arm or press against me. When I sat for breakfast he came to do this again and then gave me long searching looks as if I were not responding correctly. One day, soon after his promotion to second house-dog, when he did this I said jokingly 'say your prayers.'

Again I was rewarded with that look of incredulous joy, and he pushed his head under my arms and sat there. Now it is a daily ritual. He does it when I first sit down in the evening too. He comes, sits and looks at me, and waits for the command. His head goes down so that I can see only the top, his ears lie flat and he either pushes under my arm, or between me and the arm of the chair I am sitting in.

Praised, he feels he can now go and lie down, and be quiet, as his need for attention has been satisfied. Chita then comes for her petting, and in her turn lies down too. Josse is the first dog she has ever cuddled against. She will lie close, looking at him, and then sigh and tuck her nose into her tail, press against him and go to sleep.

She would never lie close to either Janus or Puma, and if they came close to her would get up and walk away. It's hard to know whether it is the calming effect of age, or affection that prompts her.

Within six weeks of Josse's arrival she was over her depression and swanking again. When she ran with Janus, or he walked beside me, she always had to find an immense branch and carry it. She hadn't done it much since Janus died.

Now she swaggered about the field again, showing off, carrying the biggest stick she could find, showing Josse how clever she was. He watched her, but had no desire whatever to join in the fun. He was still more interested in bird hunting.

He was rapidly becoming a most rewarding dog at home.

Elsewhere, it was a very different story.

Chapter Four

Every dog is totally different, some giving more problems than others. Janus, our Goldie, had come to me at about six months old, deaf, with tummy problems as he couldn't digest meat, and terrified of traffic, shadows and the dark.

Josse didn't like traffic either, so those training sessions with Janus long ago were useful to remember.

I took him into the village, and along the lanes. This gave rise to a problem I hadn't come across before, as Josse had been kennelled for six months, and, my vet and I suspected, had not been used to much exercise before. His very elderly owner who had died had possibly been in bad health for much of the time he owned the dog, and his subsequent kennel routine consisted of three very short walks a day, and half an hour's training once or twice a day.

I had not realised that Chita, in fact, had a great deal of exercise. Josse, trying to keep up with her, went lame within a few days of buying him.

'He's no muscle on him,' my vet said.

Again, experience with Janus was useful as he had had hip dysplasia, which is a form of inherited disability due to mis-shaping of the bone sockets. Janus often went lame, and I then treated him like a lame racehorse. First very short gentle walks, then short brisker walks, then I doubled the length of the walk, until he was fit again.

Josse had brief periods of training to heel and stay, and a couple of half-mile walks. He loved heeling, so long as he was on the lead. He trotted, tail waving, eyes watching me, eager, enjoying something that none of my other dogs had ever enjoyed. Janus would heel happily for about two minutes, but no Golden Retriever can ever take long training sessions. Chita has never liked heeling. It is too restrictive for her. She loves to use her initiative and work free from leash restraint.

I had permission to train the dogs on the disused tennis courts in the park. Here I could park my car, be fairly sure we would see no other dogs, and train first Chita, and then Josse. But as soon as the lead was taken off, Josse still streaked back to the car, desperate to get inside.

After a few days of this, I left the door open, and let him go, instead of trying to stop him. As he sat watching me, I took Chita out and played with her – running, throwing her quoit – and then knelt and cuddled her.

'Good girl. Clever girl.'

Josse couldn't bear that. He wanted petting too, and jumped out and ran to me. 'Make a fuss of me. Tell me I'm a good dog.' Chita went on to a downstay, and I did a little work with Josse, off-lead, watching him all the time. The second his head swivelled towards the car, I released him.

'In the car, then.'

Back he raced, and sat inside, in the cage I had had made for him to keep the upholstery safe. He was happy enough there and watched me, tongue lolling.

Chita was praised, released from her stay and petted, and out came Josse again. In this way the training periods off-lead could be extended, at first by half a minute at a time, and then by a whole minute, but even now, over a year later, he won't work off-lead with me in a new place for more than a few seconds, without panic setting in. In the park, which soon became part of his life, as it was of Chita's, he began to realise I wanted him back in the car, that I was not going to prevent him getting back, and that he was coming home with me every time. Training sessions there could be extended considerably.

The weekly trips to Eric had a dual purpose. I wanted the dog to learn to work in a group, with other dogs. I couldn't take him into club, as I could Chita. She would lie quietly while I taught. Josse wouldn't, as he needed to be very close to me in strange places.

I wanted him also to realise that all people didn't vanish for ever. Eric and Liz were to remain part of his life. Furthermore, he realised that he now came home with me when we visited, though I did have to leave him at Callanway when I went on

25

my annual trip South to visit friends and relatives, as he wasn't capable of fitting into any household with other dogs, and they all had dogs. That too changed with time, and recently he came with Chita to hotels and to a house where he had to stay with a Samoyed and a Rough Collie cross. He behaved very well, though we had to take great care in controlling four dogs. They endured one another but were not friends.

I tried to make several places familiar, so that he would recognise when we went there, that we would come home together, even if he did come out of the car. Visiting my friends was apt to panic him again, and when we go to a house he has never seen before it still does. The sequence had happened too often in the first months of his life and must have been etched deeply into Josse's experience.

The car drew into a drive. Strange house. Strange people. If I took out his lead, to put him on it, intending merely to walk him round their garden for exercise after a long drive in the car, he grabbed me round the waist with both paws and cried, or else held me with his mouth clamped firmly round my wrist. That never hurt me.

'Not leaving me here.'

That had already happened seven times, if we included his visit when Eric was on honeymoon. The dog would be unable to differentiate, though for the first time he had returned to a familiar place, when taken back to Callanway. Every time the dog had been put in the car, put on the lead at the end of the journey, taken out in a new place, and left behind. Those with whom he had spent the past few days disappeared for ever, never to return.

I doubt if he will ever forget that. The triggers are there to remind him, but hopefully as he becomes more and more part of our lives, he will understand that he belongs with us, and nowhere else.

The park became a source of pleasure, as training was succeeded by games, so long as there were no other dogs running free. Josse couldn't accept that, and I had no desire to turn him into a fighter. At the moment, other dogs were best avoided if they were unknown to me. Our approach to the park was greeted by excited yelps from both dogs, and Josse behaved like a normal dog so long as we kept clear of the place where he had been attacked by the Labrador. There, he still panics, even now, panting and licking his lips, trying to get into the car, afraid that some dog will race out and hurt him. The dog had been hidden by bushes and neither of us had seen it till it flew at Josse.

He is a far more submissive dog than Chita and when she bullies him, as she may if I don't watch her, he turns his head away, or comes and stands beside me, or dodges behind the car. Like Puma, he allows Chita to be the dominant dog in the family and doesn't challenge her. Janus was boss dog till he was twelve, when he gave up the struggle, as Chita had always challenged him. Josse has only stood up for himself once, when Chita finished her meal in record time and tried to finish his. He did tell her off then, and now I always watch her, as being half his weight she has half the amount he does to eat, and finishes first.

She gobbles, but Josse is an unusually slow eater for a dog as most of them gulp. Given a piece of hard crust each, Chita's appears to be inhaled. Josse takes his off to the room where he sleeps, partly to be sure she doesn't grab it, but partly because he likes to tear it up and savour it.

Again, if she does take it from him, he gives a deep sigh and comes to me for more.

The clues to his past come all the time. Puma, who had been kennelled until she was seventeen months old, when she came home with me and into a house for the first time, had had to be kept on her leash with it fastened to my belt, as everything indoors panicked her. She hated boxes – they spoke or had pictures – and she couldn't understand how a room could be light sometimes and dark at others. She loathed the vacuum cleaner.

The first time Josse saw the television set, he lay down and watched it with intense interest. He always reacts if there is a dog on the screen, and goes close to the set to stare, which probably gives him no real picture at all. If he hears the dog on the screen bark, he may run behind the set and examine its back carefully, or, if he happens to be commuting between two rooms at the time, and doesn't realise where the noise came from, or sees there is now no dog in the picture, he goes to the window and looks out. Chita is very blasée about TV, and sleeps through it. She might, occasionally, look at 'One Man and his Dog' and she was very puzzled when she herself was on TV and I switched on the programme, which had been recorded.

I wasn't sure whether she was reacting to herself or to my voice.

Josse knew about curtains which made odd swishing noises when they were drawn; he knew about vacuum cleaners, and that didn't bother him at all; he knew about doorbells, and he and Chita both reacted violently when they rang.

Yet oddly, if visitors came in the back way, and through the second door which led to the dogs' room, both rushed to the door, ignoring the strangers, being apparently unable to associate the people who were inside with the sound they had heard.

One of the drawbacks of living in an isolated place is that the dogs don't have the chance to get used to postmen, dustmen, or milkmen, as none of them come near the house. The postman, if he does have a recorded delivery parcel, won't get out of his van, but hoots for me to come. He is terrified of German Shepherds.

Visitors being infrequent, the dogs have no chance to get used to them. A visitor is a great event to be greeted with an uproarious din. It is very convenient if I have canvassers, or people trying to sell me tarmac, but it isn't at all useful when friends call.

In those early days Josse had to be put on the lead and led to greet the newcomers once they were seated, as he not only rushed at them barking, but he nipped. Not a dangerous bite, but a very naughty puppy nip that bruised. He did it twice, during his first three months with us, and that had to be stopped.

I put him on the lead as soon as the doorbell rang. Kenneth let the visitors in, to be greeted by Chita with excitement but not dangerously and then Josse was led in. Visitors were provided with dog biscuits, and once they had fed him, he relaxed.

There was no further problem till it was time for them to go, when he became very excited again, and rushed around barking, and I was afraid he might nip in his excitement. So that visitors leaving necessitated more training. 'Dogs, down.' They have to stay down until the visitors are outside and the front door shut again. It was over six months before Josse could be trusted to greet people sensibly. The sessions were much easier with dog-minded friends. In the end, if non-dog people were there, the dogs were put in the car. People who don't understand dogs don't always co-operate, or see why they should. The dogs ought to behave without any training at all!

It is impossible to make people who have never lived with dogs understand that dogs have to be taught how to cope with all kinds of situations, and that to them every new person creates a new and different situation.

Thinking this over, I devised another kind of training session, with the front door wide open and dogs on a sitstay in the hall, not allowed to move until I told them. This requires time and concentration, but it does prevent a wild explosion when the door is opened, as they never know whether they are going to be led through and allowed outside, or have to stay where they are.

It means I must remember as dogs don't understand 'sometimes'. They understand 'all' or 'nothing'. A dog allowed on the bed when he is clean, and smacked for getting up there when he has muddy paws can never work out why he is wrong today but was right yesterday. He doesn't realise he is now muddy.

The training had hidden benefits. It means I can unload the car with the dogs lying quietly in the porch and the door open. It means I can go out of the back door and put rubbish in the bin without two dogs flying out with me. It does not yet mean they will sit patiently when visitors come, as that doesn't happen often enough, but they will sit when Liz comes, as she comes daily, and she is no longer greeted by a tremendous leaping rush which is very hard to control.

Chita always excites when Liz puts on her coat to go, and races round screaming. She always had to be stopped. She never remembered. Josse, told to sit still while Liz went, did, and Chita, after realising he got praised and she got scolded, sat with him. Now both dogs stay while Liz goes and life is far quieter. I had never before thought of turning Liz's departure into a training routine. It didn't matter so much with one dog. Janus, being deaf, had never heard the carry-on, and never joined in. He stayed at my feet in my study while Chita tried to follow Liz out into the garden. She did stop when made to but now she doesn't even start her nonsense.

The dogs know Liz so well that if we are out when she comes, she can let herself in with the key, and be greeted as if she were a family member.

Training to behave for living, as well as for competition, is vital, as there is always the time when a crisis occurs, and an untrained dog may add to it. There may be a small child outside with his parents who would be terrified by an explosion of dogs through that door to the garden. Once the routine is established, they are more likely to obey a quick command, and save not only confusion, because they don't know what is expected of them, but possible damage to people as well. Small dogs are far easier to manage. The large breeds must be trained for maximum control.

This year three of our club dogs have been run over. They flew out of the house and then through the garden gate, which a tradesman had left open. One was dragged and severely injured; one had a broken pelvis and is now lame; and the third was killed. It happens so fast and so easily.

It is much easier to control one dog than two. Janus had been old while Chita was young, and hadn't caused me this kind of problem. Chita, in spite of her years, is neither staid nor calm and can still be a handful. A second dog was causing her to revert to some of her puppy silliness. Having Josse was making me think over everything we did. Much had become part of Chita's life and I didn't need to remind her. Ordinary household routine, so long as it doesn't involve the exciting expectation of running free in the garden, is easy. In eight years she *had* learned to obey some rules: she knew she was supposed to lie quietly when people visited, that she mustn't rush around when grandchildren come, as they are tiny. Josse had it all to learn.

The years between two and three are maturing years. One

big advantage with an adult dog is that he learns far more quickly than a pup can and remembers. Puppy memories are short and at eight months, when they start to mature, the training is all to do again, as now they begin to challenge everything, wanting pack leader position in the family. Josse was so receptive that I saw improvements in many directions quite quickly, so long as neither his chasing instinct, nor his guarding instinct were involved. He was past the age of challenge, but like all dogs he is an opportunist and will take advantage if he can.

Now when I get up, both dogs are sitting, waiting at the door of the room where they sleep. As I open it, they greet me very happily, weaving round me, making small moaning noises, tails waving ecstatically. Chita has learned that from Josse, as if she leaped at me, as she is apt to do if not checked, he was praised. She wasn't. They then run ahead to the back door, but come back repeatedly to greet me again. There is none of the initial wild rush that occurred when Josse first came indoors. I had to check it, as he knocked me against the door and his claws scratched my face as he leaped at me, and Chita ran around crazily, squealing for her share of attention. So training began for some sense there too. Out of the door, call 'sit', through it, and if they weren't sitting when I opened it, I shut it again. 'No. Sit.' In the end they began to understand, and now I enjoy meeting them without any fear of being damaged in the process.

The back door is opened and they look at me. Can we go out? That took months to train, but was well worth the effort. Outside is so exciting and every dog wants to rush through an open door.

That training was relatively simple. If they rushed at the door instead of listening to my command to sit, I opened it a crack, and shut it again. I might do that ten times. In the end it dawned on them that they weren't going out until they did as they were told. They sat, while I checked outside. We have stray cats, and I don't want them harmed – or the dogs getting hurt by scratching dogs.

I had to remember every time, as what dogs remember is the time you forget, and the training has to start again.

31

'Go and be good.' Off they go, down into the long grass, sniffing to see if the weasel was out last night, or if the pheasants have been on our side of the fence. One morning Josse was a particularly long time, standing with his nose buried deep in the unmown grass. When I went to see what he was doing, he was finishing off the last of the partridges' eggs, as the silly birds nest, every year, on the ground, beside the dogs' jumps. They lay another clutch, not learning, and the dogs revel in an extra meal, as I never find the nest in time, and the dogs do need to be able to run free in our own garden.

Some mornings the pheasants are on our side of the fence. This is irritating as Josse is an inveterate bird chaser. So far it is one vice I haven't yet cured, though we are working on it.

One morning there were six birds there, a cock and five hens. I could see their heads as they walked along the remains of an old ditch that is lower than the rest of that part of the garden. As we live on the side of a hill there are several levels, which is very good for dogs' muscles.

I did not want Josse to chase, so before I let the dogs out I clapped my hands. The birds ignored me. They are used to gunfire, and appear not to associate it with danger to them. Our neighbour lets his shooting rights. I slammed the door, but that had no effect either. The dogs needed to go out, so I let them, hoping they would fail to see the birds.

Chita didn't see them. She went out and came in. Josse was just turning to come in when the cock saw him and sounded his warning. That tremendous clanging gonglike note is enough to startle any animal within hearing. Josse spun round, saw the birds and raced off.

I called.

He was deaf.

The hens, wiser than the cock, scurried in an undignified huddle and crept under the five-barred gate.

The cock flew.

So did my dog.

For one startling moment I saw the bird in flight and Josse leaping high off the ground, with his head within inches of that long tempting tail. The bird managed to gain height and land, indignantly, on the other side of the fence. Josse raced along the fence, trying to bash his way through. Foiled, he tried to crawl under the gate, but fortunately the gap was too small. By then I had reached him, and made him behave. A shake, and the command, 'heel' in a tone that made him realise I meant it.

He followed me in, his tongue hanging out, his eyes bright with remembered mischief. Cor, I enjoyed that.

Maybe, but something had to be done. The problem being what, as pheasants don't appear to order. These had learned their lesson and never appeared again on our side of that fence.

Chapter Five

By now it seemed obvious to me that Josse had almost certainly been brought up in a town, for country sights triggered him to constant misbehaviour. If he hadn't, an ageing and weary owner must have allowed him to run riot where game and stock were concerned.

Our neighbour runs bullocks on the marsh field as we can't get mowers on to it. Mervyn had four beauties, enchanting little animals only twelve weeks old. A Welsh black, a Hereford, and two Friesians. Across the narrow river, within sight, are six Charollaises, all being fattened up for beef. They are usually sold in their second year.

Eric has bullocks as neighbours, and Josse was used to those. But they are separated from the dogs by a high wall, and can only be seen if they put their heads over, though they are plainly visible to humans. Also these were steady animals, not frisky calves.

Off-lead, Josse fence-ran the bullocks, barking at them, becoming more and more excited. The bullocks in their turn ran in terror from the barking dog, making him even worse. For weeks lessons had to be on a line. 'No', snatch, and heel the dog away. Over and over, until I dreamed about training him.

He wouldn't be cured until I could let him off and know he would ignore the bullocks. It became imperative that this was made top priority, as those bullocks wouldn't put on any weight if they were constantly being raced along the fence, and they hadn't the sense to go away. They simply ran alongside, ahead of him, and whether it was a game or panic didn't matter. They still wouldn't fatten.

It was ten weeks before I dared let Josse off-lead when the bullocks were in the field. There is only pigwire between dog and cattle, so there is no way they can be hidden from him.

Since the field is small, they don't graze it regularly, which means it is used for two weeks, then left empty for two weeks to allow the grass to grow.

Josse would get used to an empty field, and then, quite suddenly, the cattle were back. The Hereford in particular was extremely inquisitive and quite likely to thrust his head over the fence. The bullocks grew used to the dog sooner than he did to them. Nowadays he is rarely triggered to run them, though if they do have a mad moment and canter about, especially on a windy day, he may race to the fence and bark, but will stop the second he hears my voice.

Just to make life really complicated, the top field beyond our garden, which is separated from us by pigwire as well, is re-enforced by a Leylandii hedge on our side, behind which the dogs can hide from me for several minutes, running there unseen between the back of the trees and the fence. This didn't matter until our neighbour, unknown to me, bought a donkey. One afternoon there was the dickens of a shindy, with dogs barking and donkey braying. Josse was learning not to run bullocks, but donkeys aren't bullocks, and dogs have to learn that they too must not be fence-run either.

Donk brayed his displeasure very noisily and continuously. When he felt like giving vent to his feelings, he could be heard quite easily, even from Maes y Porth, the farm where we track, which is a mile away. Close to, the noise was incredible. Turning his back to the fence, he kicked out. He couldn't reach Josse, and for a few hectic minutes, neither could I, as I can't get behind those trees. The dog emerged to find a better vantage point and I managed to grab his collar and hang on. Chita had decided – as I was obviously not pleased – that it would be wiser to lie down, as she did whenever Josse managed to get through to Chia's quarters and chase the cat. 'I'm a good girl, I am.' There have been donkeys or horses off and on in that field several times during her life and she had been well drilled. And once, in her salad days, chasing a goat, she had also encountered the electric fence which prevented the goat from wandering. She had leaped in the air and then bolted, and I suspected she now felt there was likely to be one of those strange painful invisible barriers round any sort of farm animal.

35

It was no more fun for the donkey to be tormented than for the bullocks, so we had morning sessions immediately after breakfast on the long-line beside the bullock field, and late in the afternoon we did our donkey training.

One afternoon when Donk, who was only a baby, was especially active and noisy, Chita, much to my surprise, was triggered by him too, and as I finished Josse's lesson, she suddenly raced up to the trees, and behind them, and as he kicked out, she barked.

Two lots of long-lining were no fun at all, so for the next two weeks, every afternoon, I weeded the bank, which is a mass of heathers, and is within a few feet of that field, with both dogs on downstay. If either of them moved, back they had to come, immediately, and each day they were put nearer and nearer the donkey.

At last came the day when I could relax. Neither dog took the slightest notice of either Donk or the cattle. It was easily seven months before I could trust Josse completely and let him roam at will when the cattle were in the field, keeping an eye on him, but able to turn my back. The donkey had left by then, as that field is minute, and he went to fresh grazing.

There wasn't as much time as I would have liked for town training, or for park training. There weren't enough hours in the day. Josse was learning but he had so much to learn.

Many people I know feel chasing doesn't really matter and let – or even encourage – their dogs to chase stray cats off their property and are then astounded when one day the dog catches the cat and kills it. The dog thinks that's what it's meant to do.

Others let their dogs chase rabbits and hares, saying it's easy enough to cure. But it isn't. It's extremely difficult to break any habit that's been allowed to develop. It is far easier to prevent it when the puppy is very young and much more manageable, as the cure takes so much time and dedication.

That fact was becoming only too plain in that Josse's habit of racing to the car if anything at all bothered him was becoming worse if anything. Once he began pulling, I was off balance and had no choice but to hang on and follow. Once at the car I walked away, and he had to come too but as soon as we turned, he dived again. He was, I suspected, terrified that this time he would not be allowed in the car, that he would be left behind, and so he had to make absolutely sure he reached it and got inside. Once there, he relaxed.

In that respect he was far from being an easy dog. He was a very difficult dog, and it was one thing that he simply would not learn, as panic overrode sense, and dominated him. I had to cure the problem, or one day we might be parked on the wrong side of a main road, and he would hurtle across, and one or both of us would die under some vehicle. I did not dare park in any place where that was even a faint possibility, and that meant he was only getting taught in fairly isolated areas where we could park very safely, and walk away from roads. Yet he needed to meet people, traffic, and other dogs.

I had to devise a method of dealing with that as it couldn't be allowed to continue. The trouble was, how on earth to stop it.

Chapter Six

Although Josse was a new experience for me, we had had a number of re-homed dogs in club over the years. Laddie, a big German Shepherd, had been bought as a stud dog, but had grown too big. He was sold as a pet when he was two. He was an odd dog, very gentle, very kind, very biddable, and much too good.

He had always lived in a kennel, but soon adapted to the house. He learned his exercises, but always had about him an air that said 'I'll do it because you say so, but honestly, humans are silly!'

He had lived with his new owner for over a year before he relaxed and became a normal dog. Sue came in one evening beaming. 'Laddie was really naughty today,' she said. He had chased a cat, refused to come when called, and then, after being scolded for tearing up the morning newspaper, had reacted happily to his training lesson. I greeted him, and he bounced at me, wagging his tail, as if he had only just discovered how dogs should behave. He had spent his days alone in kennels except for brief exercise, and had no idea when bought how to run wild or to play.

Jed had been far more difficult, as he had been the victim of a man who had kicked, starved and beaten him. He came to club a thin, poor-coated, miserable dog, that shook if any man came near him. Women, however, could cuddle him. Within six months he was beautiful, a big handsome Collie, with a dense coat.

We could never pick up even a pencil near him. It was two years before he would allow any man, even his owner's husband, to stroke him. Five years later he is still wary of strange men.

Sajo had been a police dog. He was found tied by a thick rope to a post at the edge of the hard shoulder on the M1. He was about a year old, and not surprisingly was terrified. He became a very good working dog, but never again could he be tied up while his handler attended to some duty, nor could he be left alone on an out-of-sight downstay. They always took care that such situations did not arise.

Sajo is dead now, but even as an old dog, tying up terrified him, and he fought the rope and cried. It was only tried once, when his handler forgot, as the dog had been with him for eight years, and he himself had forgotten this was something they must never do with Sajo.

I didn't want to own a dog that, all his life, bolted to my car when we were away from it.

I took Josse to the vet again. He was still stressed by strange places, and the vet's surgery stressed him too. He obeyed the command to sit, while he was examined, but he shook and licked his lips constantly, and he was wary, ready to leap into action, whether to protect me or himself I didn't know.

Extreme stress was diagnosed, but we felt it better to try and conquer it without any drugs. Neither my vet nor I like artificial aids to recovery unless they are really necessary. I hate pills and avoid them if I can.

I had learned to recognise the symptoms, though different dogs show stress differently. It was that stress, due to the fear of being handed over again, I was sure, that induced that wild race back to the car whenever we were away from it. It didn't matter where we were. Lessons at Eric's were likely to induce it quickly and at first I didn't enjoy them at all. But, as the dog began to realise he always returned with me, we could work for the full hour with the other ten dogs, and he made great progress. As I had more dog experience than the rest of the class, I did too, which boosted my morale. I never do have much self-confidence, but have to work hard at that, too.

The walk down the lane, after the lesson, was never a leisurely stroll, and the last few yards was still a panic rush, but it was getting better. Out in the park, or visiting friends, or in the car-park by the beach, he still flew back, whether off-lead or on. He loved the beach, where we only walk in winter, but as soon as we turned around to go home, he was off. 'Must get to the car, must get in. I'm safe in the car.' He might not always be safe *en route* to the car.

I walked him away; I snatched the lead; I made him sit.

It made no difference.

It was painful as he pulled my arm. It alarmed anyone who happened to be near as he charged past them, panting. He ignored anything in the way, and I had to be very careful to make sure our path to the car was unimpeded. I could exercise him without worrying that someone might get knocked down by his rush, in lonely places, but that would mean he could never come to a show and Trials would be out of the question. It would add immeasureably to his life if he could come out and about like a normal dog. It was also restricting Chita.

I puzzled for some time as to the way to cure this. One day I took the car to a very big car-park in Menai Bridge. I found a space at the edge, with no other cars near us. I had a bag of titbits with me. Josse had been taught not to leap out as soon as the car door was opened. He stood patiently as I slipped the chain over his head.

'OK. Out,' I said.

He came out and looked about him. He had never been here before. At once he panicked, and his front paws went round my waist, his mouth seized my hand and he held on, tight. A woman waiting in a nearby car looked astounded.

I didn't move away from the car. I persuaded him to sniff the titbit. He released me, and took it, and I told him to sit, right beside the car, the door to his cage open.

Chita was crying to come out. 'Not fair, he has all the fun.' Josse would have preferred not to get out of the car at all. She was longing to be free, and come and work with me. She still travelled in front with me, and was pressed against the window, watching.

Josse sat. We didn't go anywhere. We stayed right there. He watched me, expecting that we would walk away from the car, but we didn't.

'OK. In the car.'

He looked at me in disbelief, and then jumped in, his tail

wagging. He hadn't been taken away from the car, he hadn't been prevented in any way from getting back to the car, as there had been no tension on his lead. He had been encouraged to get in.

I stood back from the car, at the end of his leash, and held out a titbit.

'Out. Good dog. Sit. Good dog.'

He was given the titbit. His eyes brightened and his tail wagged. 'In, good boy.' Titbit. 'Out, good boy. Sit, good boy.' Titbit. He began to relax completely. This in/out game was fun, and he wasn't being asked to leave his sanctuary, or go anywhere.

The titbits were tiny, little cat-munch biscuits, and Josse loved them.

He went in and out ten times and then I moved him a few paces from the car, back to the car before he realised we had turned, at a sober pace, sit, and in.

I could maybe have forced him over the months to do as I wanted, but forcing only added to stress, and this was a dog that had broken down under training once already (with his fifth owner, the man who had bought him from the RSPCA). No dog will train well or be reliable if he is made to work through fear, and this, to Josse, was a kind of work. It involved commands, and it involved obedience, even if it wasn't the kind of obedience one trains to perform in a show ring.

Often not even people who show continuously realise that those ring commands work in everyday situations too. Heel, no matter what is happening around you.

Sit, and let that very old lady pass you without the fear you may leap up and knock her down. Sit at the kerb, and the drivers know we aren't going to race across the road, out of control.

Find my car keys, or tell me if that's my golf ball or if it belongs to the man who says it's his. That is what the scent exercises are about. So that ring training goes on alongside everyday training and the better the dog obeys ring commands the better he obeys everyday commands made to suit everyday circumstances.

41

'Stay in the car; don't jump out.' That way dogs can get killed and one that was killed had worked at Cruft's, but the stay training had never been applied to cars.

Someone wrote to me recently saying 'I have obedience dogs, but not *obedient* dogs,' but that's silly, as if they obey in the ring they must surely obey the same commands outside it. Sit instead of flying through the door. Sit, instead of leaping up at me. Sit, instead of chewing that shoe. Good dog! No need to grumble. He's earned praise instead.

While we were learning that dogs don't race at cars we were also learning ring routines. So we practised stays by the car, instead of in the park, and when Josse jumped out he had to come to the front of me and sit, waiting for his reward, learning the ring recall, without being aware that this, too, was a form of dog drill.

After a few minutes of this I let Josse rest and took Chita out and heeled her off-lead round the car-park. It wasn't the place I would have chosen for our afternoon exercise, but Josse had to learn to meet the world, and he wasn't going to learn that in the deserted lanes at Maes y Porth where we rarely met anyone. We went there afterwards. The dogs would run free and had the great pleasure of fields and woods.

I changed our routine and our training completely. This, after all, was training too. The next afternoon we went to the other car-park in Menai Bridge and practised the same routine. Josse was never more than three feet from the car. He had no opportunity to race to it, and the door remained open, so that he knew he could get in at a second's notice.

By the end of the week he was managing a sitstay on the lead, ten feet from that open door. A quiet walk back, a sit by the door before he was allowed to get in, and then his titbit reward, which was now a big dog biscuit that he could chew happily while Chita had her exercise and training.

She is easy to exercise adequately as she will race after her quoit for ever and could have more energetic running when we reached home.

The weeks went by. Josse could walk round Menai Bridge and return to the car-park, sitstay away from the car, and then we could walk back soberly, Josse behaving like a normal dog.

That was in car-parks. Back in the park, with mown lawns and flower-beds and narrow tarmac paths, I thought I could walk him, and then Chita. I went beyond his tolerance limit, and suddenly realised the car was out of sight, though we, in fact, were not far away. It was masked by bushes. Panic set in, and I realised Josse's new habit was broken. It would be triggered, far too easily, by something unknown to me, that upset the dog, and made him feel insecure again.

The same teaching needed to be done here, and probably would in almost any other place I chose to park in. It might get easier over the years. It might not. It might be a part of Josse I had to accept, as that constant change of owner had maybe marred him in that respect for life.

I began to work out distances; to train Josse all the time within sight of the car, to leave the door open on the old tennis courts, so that he could run back, but on *my* command.

Downstay, with the car twenty yards away. Even with Chita beside him, he never took his eyes off that car. But by the autumn he would walk to it, off-lead, beside me, sit when we reached it and wait for a command to get in. At last we were making headway.

· Even at Eric's training centre, Josse began to behave better and not rush to the car. The problem, I thought, was solved. I thought wrong, as dog problems are rarely solved easily. Some never go. Others are masked, and may be there all the time, unseen, apparently forgotten, to surface suddenly, brought back again by something that the dog appreciates but that we never will. The underlying cause remains a mystery, as we can't talk to dogs, and we can never, with a rescued dog, or a dog that has had several homes, know every thing that has happened in the past.

Chapter Seven

Eric and I discussed Josse endlessly when I visited, as well as the other dogs he was training. There is so much to learn, and every dog makes the owner, or the trainer, realise that new ways of teaching this particular dog must be sought, in order to overcome a specific fault that has never been met before in any other dog.

Josse was learning over the weeks that he came with me when I left Eric and that even if he didn't, I came back. He was left there twice in his first few months with me. I felt he might be afraid he was going to be left behind if we went to strange houses and hotels and that would make him very difficult indeed.

We made his first experience of being left at Callanway a very brief one. Eric and Liz had been married in Durham, which was too far away for most of his friends. So they gave a reception for all those who had been unable to make the journey. It was on a Sunday, as most people worked, and it was one of the few fine days in the summer of 1985.

The farmhouse was a fairly new acquisition; the builders were making a new drive, putting up new kennel blocks, and the place generally had an air of impermanence. That day, however, there was an air of festivity. Everything had been made as tidy as possible, the unfinished patio was decked with flowers in containers that hung all round, and the lane where we walked the dogs had been marked out so that cars could be parked easily.

I stayed at the Ellesmere Hotel in Macclesfield the night before. Chita and I always have the same room. I called briefly at the kennels, and left Josse behind. He was in his old kennel. When I arrived next day, in the early afternoon, I took him for a walk, and then put him back in my car with Chita. This was, hopefully, to make him realise that, although I left him, I would return and fetch him again. He was to stay there for three weeks, starting a couple of weeks later, while I went South and this was a preliminary.

Eric works his dog, Fonz, in police dog Trials. They do so well together that Fonz recently won a Championship Certificate and the pair were invited to compete at the Metropolitan Police Dogs Open Day, in the civilian Police Dog stake. This is a rare honour, offered to very few civilians. Eric and Fonz came second.

So all his friends tended to either work in civilian police dog Trials, or were working police dog handlers. There were faces I knew from Trials, although I didn't know their owners well, as they worked much higher stakes than Chita and I.

The talk was of dogs: of Trials, of dogs that had become champions; of tracks that were successful, and of tracks that failed; of judges and their peculiarities; of the silly things that often happened, as nothing is more unpredictable than working with a dog on a moor or near woods.

I had completely lost Chita's attention in Tatton Park in her early days as a Trials dog when a herd of deer came over the hill. She had never seen deer before. She tracked deer instead of tracking properly, and so did many other dogs. That day had been so unsuccessful that the park was never used for Trials again. There had been a radio-controlled plane rally there as well, and small planes, buzzing above our heads, whizzing and zooming and diving, were alarming, especially as we felt they might get out of control and land on or near a dog, and hurt or terrify it.

There was no fear of any such hazard at Callanway. It is very isolated, with just one close neighbour, and every member of that family, including the children, was there. The only outside distraction was likely to come from ramblers, as the right of way goes through a field alongside Eric's fields.

Neither Eric nor Liz were interested in a conventional wedding reception. We had all been told to arrive in our dog working clothes, to bring our dogs, and not to forget our wellingtons. The only conventional part of the day was the very splendid buffet, made by friends.

We were to have a Working Trial fun day. Since all these

45

were experienced, highly trained dogs, it was possible to take liberties with the Trials routines that couldn't have been taken with a part-trained dog. It would have confused it badly. No Trials was ever like this, either. The day was set aside for fun and fun we were going to have. The dogs seemed to know it too and were all eager to join in the games. Most were working the civilian Police Dog stake. Chita and Liz's Sheena were by no means up to that standard, but both were used to training and competition and had far more experience than the average family dog would have had.

All responded easily to control words, and could be brought from excitement back to sense again within seconds. None of them was on-lead but when a dog was not working it was told to lie at its handler's feet, and watch the working dog. They worked singly, but otherwise any Trials rule was there to be broken!

The Trials search is based, as is most of the Trials work, on police dog work. It is a mock hunt for murder clues. The ground may be farmland, plough or pasture; it may be a common, or woodland. The square in the Utility Dog stake, which is the first stake with a track in it, is twenty-five yards each side, marked by a pole at each corner.

If there are thirty dogs, there will be thirty separate squares, as no dog searches the same square as any other dog. There will also be thirty sets of four articles; each dog must have the same type of articles. These should be the size of a matchbox, and may be any set of a considerable variety. Chita has found half beer-mats, pieces of carpets about three inches square, sparkplugs, a six-inch nail, a large key, cartridge cases, a small tangle of baler twine, a section of rope, a strip of leather, among many other rather odd objects, known to Triallers as 'articles'.

At one Trials Eric had gathered together a nut and bolt, a small bag containing sugar which was supposed to be drugs, a hypodermic syringe, and a key-ring for each of his handlers. This simulated a real situation in which a break-in had been carried out by a drug addict in search of supplies. He had broken the bolt to get in, and dropped various articles as

46

he ran away, having been disturbed while in the act of committing his crime.

Each dog has four minutes in which to search the square and bring the articles to the handler, one by one. Most dogs love this and it's very useful to teach – in real life my dogs have found my car keys, any number of gloves, my wedding ring, and a hotel key that I had dropped in long grass while walking them when staying away from home. The handler is not allowed in the square. Should he step in he loses marks.

Two squares were marked out, and we were divided into teams, one team under Les Edwards, who is a trainer of police dog handlers. I was in that. The other team was under Terry Hadley, very well known both as competitor and judge. There were five handlers and dogs in each team. There were twenty articles in each square, and each dog had to find four; it was run as a mixture of a search and a relay race. None of the dogs had ever worked that way before, but it was soon evident that they were enjoying it as much as we were.

It was also evident that not only were the usual rules to be broken, so that handlers could go into the square, see an article and pick it up, but that both teams were going to cheat like mad. It was almost impossible to command the dogs because we were all laughing so much, and the noise on the sidelines as the spectators who either didn't have dogs, or weren't in that particular game cheered us, became incredible.

In went the first dog, found one article and brought it out, and then cast round unsuccessfully. As it put its head down Les leaped into the square (which isn't allowed in Trials,) and picked up two articles. Dog found two; Les found two. 'Four,' he shouted, 'next dog in.' Next dog was Chita who found three, two of which were torn in two when they reached Les who was collecting, and had picked up a fourth. 'Eleven articles,' he yelled, 'next dog in.'

Eleven (out of eight!) wasn't bad going but Terry's team had thirteen out of eight, so the next four articles we found were all divided into two and one into three.

By the end of the time most of us were helpless with laughter. Our team lost as we only had thirty articles out of twenty while Terry's team had forty, everyone having cheated like mad.

47

Everyone was letting their hair down, and that without any alcohol whatever. We were to drink the newly weds' health later.

Every dog then had to do a sendaway; Chita by now had decided the day wasn't like anything she had known before and made a lovely mess of hers, racing out in quite the wrong direction, by now full of fun herself, and so did Liz's Sheena. Sendaway is a basic police dog exercise, so that those dogs doing the civilian Police Dog stakes excelled, and it was lovely to watch the dog run at top speed away from the handler on command and drop as if shot when told.

A police dog may be sent to a gap in a wall many yards from the handler to intercept a running crook, so the exercise has a lot of point. It is also an exercise which can be used to practise putting the fast-running dog down, at a single command, so that if it is chasing a child, or a sheep or a cat, it can be dropped and the chase is aborted.

At one point in the afternoon Eric brought out a lovely little German Shepherd bitch he had in for sale. She proved to be a Houdini, and managed to climb the kennel wall and try to get out, when he first had her. She was unbelievably agile, adored jumping and jumped through Eric's arms, over his raised leg, into his arms, over his back, with the makings of a wonderful stunt dog. Everyone pretended to be vastly impressed by Eric's stunts. Isn't he clever? How ever did you manage to teach *that*? In fact, all their dogs could do the tricks too. Jody was an inexperienced youngster, just learning the rudiments of stuntwork.

The afternoon passed unbelievably fast, and then it was time to go in to eat. The dogs went into the cars, and we were all about to go indoors.

To everyone's amazement Liz erupted from the house, clutching Eric's wallet, shouting, 'I've had enough. I'm leaving him. I'm sick of dogs,' and sped across the field we had just been working on. Eric, behind her, had Dusty, his brood bitch, with him and said, 'After her. She's got the housekeeping money,' and off went Dusty, running to hold Liz's arm and detain her.

After our first initial surprise there was a roar of laughter, as

Eric went to her, and they walked back together with their arms around one another, Dusty leaping at Liz to lick her hands. 'Dogs are very useful,' he said.

Indoors, the food was delicious and by now the party was going with a tremendous swing. There were several children there, and Les took tenpenny pieces out of their ears and performed other conjuring tricks, fascinating them. By the time it was dark nobody wanted to go home, and Les and Terry vied with each other telling jokes. They were the funniest jokes I had ever heard, told brilliantly, each trying to outdo the other, but not one single joke was unfit for a child to hear.

Other wedding receptions tend to blur in memory, but none of us will ever forget Liz and Eric's.

Chapter Eight

One thing that is certain with any dog is that learning doesn't happen overnight. With a dog that has had a bad start it is a very slow process indeed, as those past habits have to be eliminated, past fears have to be alleviated, and the dog has to be taught a whole new way of life.

Josse's first owner may have allowed him to lie on his bed, or the settee. I don't know. Josse did learn fast that that is not allowed in our home. Some new ways were easy for him. Others very difficult indeed.

He slipped backwards as far as walking in the town or the park went while I was on holiday. Three weeks is a long time in a dog's life. I wished I hadn't had to leave him then, as when we returned home the desire to reach the car fast was stronger than ever, and I had to go back to the beginning of the training, to reassure him. I had only had him just over a month when we went away. That holiday had been booked before I bought the dog.

I decided to start training him for Trials, as well as Obedience competition, even if we never made it. It would give him something new to learn, and he might well enjoy jumping.

Chita is a natural jumper. Puppies aren't supposed to jump, as it's bad for their legs. Nobody told me how I should anchor a pup that jumped over my legs, jumped over the other dogs, jumped over anything that was in her way, and preferred to jump up a three-foot bank rather than go over or round it.

My real problem with her was never to teach her to jump, but to restrict her jumping, or she cleared walls and gates and trespassed, and with sheep around that would be far from popular.

Josse was very different. He regarded the jumps with bewilderment. He barged into the hurdle, even when it was only nine inches off the ground, or knocked it down. He seemed to have no spring and no desire whatever to lift himself into the air. Janus had never jumped, but he had bad hips. He could never even jump into the car; he had to climb in with an effort and an undignified scramble, and my hands under his rump to lift him. I had Josse examined. Nothing wrong with him at all. He simply couldn't understand how to move his body to leap over that obstacle.

I changed the hurdle, which consisted of two posts and a movable bar and brought out one of those I had had made for the course I was planning to run in the autumn. This was solid at the bottom, with two wide planks of wood painted white. Josse did realise he couldn't walk through it, and he did a peculiar bump over, just clearing it.

I tried throwing something for him to fetch, but as he wouldn't pick anything up either, that didn't work. Chita loved retrieving over the hurdle. Josse didn't like jumping. He didn't like retrieving. He didn't like strange places. It didn't look as if we would ever make Trials.

He only came up to the jumps if I put him on the lead. Off-lead, he ran off, as he had done in his heelwork when I first brought him home. That was now conquered so long as I kept every session very short indeed. Could we conquer his lack of desire to jump?

Apart from anything else it is a good way of exercising the dogs and Chita finds it such fun it seemed a shame that he should be deprived of something that might give him pleasure.

One sunny afternoon I had both dogs with me, and was gardening. I found a long-lost quoit of Chita's among the weeds, and threw it over the hurdle, which was at three feet, as I had been training Chita earlier that afternoon. Josse felt lazy and lay there, watching. He is a much less active dog than Chita, though recently she had been far less energetic and I wondered if she were ill. After examination, the vet pointed out there was nothing wrong with her; she was as active as any five-year-old dog, but at almost nine years old not even she was capable of perpetual motion, though she had been in the past.

Chita saw the quoit flung, and raced over the hurdle, grabbed the toy and jumped back to me. Josse, triggered to movement by her sudden run, raced after her, found the hurdle in his way,

51

and cleared it from a standing jump, like a cat, without any effort at all.

As he had apparently been unable to manage nine inches, this astonished me. We had been struggling with that baby jump for days.

I took Chita back to the hurdle, threw the quoit, intending her to jump this time, and sent her over. Josse followed again, and turned his head to look at me as he landed. 'Clever dog.' It was very easy to be enthusiastic. Quite suddenly, he had realised what was wanted, and from that day on was very happy indeed to go over the hurdle. He never looks as if he is actually going to jump. He approaches nonchalently, his body far looser and more gangling than Chita's. He appears not to look at the obstacle at all, and not even to be concentrating, and then, just as I am sure he can't possibly manage to jump, he soars into the air. When he came to Worthing with me just over a year later, he jumped the paddock fence – which is more than four feet high – from a standing start, in order to join me. Chita hurls herself at any obstacle, gathering speed, and soars over. Josse flips over.

It took six weeks to teach him to hurdle accurately. From there we progressed to the long jump which is never so easy. He did not like it. He went round it; he jumped the corner; he landed on the middle of it, although I had made it only about eighteen inches wide.

'Long jumping was difficult,' he said. 'Impossible,' he said, until one day, running free, he came to a wide puddle and rather than splash through, he cleared it. That seemed to unlock another block in his brain, as next day when we came to try the long jump, he did clear it, and gradually that too could be lengthened.

All went well until we reached five feet. That day, he misjudged it, and hit his hind paws on the last plank. It is made up of five planks, which are angled in such a way that they appear from a dog's eye view to make a continuous sloping ramp.

It was some weeks before I could even persuade him to try again, but gradually he overcame that fear. Josse hates being hurt so much that any small bang will set him back. Chita is oblivious of pain, and if she catches the end plank, her attitude says 'oh damn it,' and she will come back and make sure she clears it next time.

The scale presented problems too. No way was he going over that. Again it was Chita who triggered him: she was lying down one day, watching a session with Josse, during which I cajoled and coaxed, and tried holding a large piece of sausage over the planks, which were set at four feet, and not at six. Chita was unable to stand any more, and flew over, grabbing at the titbit. Josse was so indignant at losing his food that he followed her, and from that day began to scale too.

Now, a year later, the Trials agility apparatus is part of his life, though we have not yet achieved nine feet with the long jump.

Chita had passed her last veterinary examination with flying colours and though she was older than most dogs in Trials, there was no need to retire her yet. In fact it would be a shame to do so as retired dogs, like retired people, grow depressed, feeling they are redundant. Old gundogs and old police dogs yearn to be back on the job again and become very bright indeed if they are allowed to use their skills, even if the dogs are slow and their skills are rusty.

I was tracking with Chita, and had gone back to little tracks as she had been making mistakes. She had also lost interest. So every track she did had something exciting at the end of it, much more exciting than her usual toy, and since it was Chita, who is still difficult in some ways, and won't co-operate unless she is really stimulated, her end article was food. It might be a crust of brown bread, which she has a craving for, or a piece of chicken, or a sausage.

This was much more worthwhile than a cartridge case, or a piece of leather or a small piece of stick, and it only took a few days to switch her excitement on again. People are odd about food. The Americans use it for tracking as a matter of course, but in this country, it is frowned on.

Some say if you use it and the dog finds it not there once, it will cease to track. That isn't true, as the dog will always do several tracks without a food incentive, and once it has learned to love tracking for its own sake, the food isn't needed any more. A disappointing track that goes wrong can often be remedied with a track that ends in food afterwards and one of the best trackers I met, a little Yorkie, was taught to track by having his dinner laid at the end of the track, and having to hunt for it.

This may sound mean, but dogs do hunt for their food and all he was being asked to do was earn his meal. He loved that daily chore which ended in a fantastic reward. His dinner!

Some days we tracked for food, once Chita was interested again; some days for her toy and a game. It didn't matter which, in the end. She would work for either. As soon as I had a keen dog tracking again I decided to introduce Josse to tracking too.

He regarded the harness with extreme suspicion, as he always does anything new to him. I put Chita's on her, and let her run around in it. Hers was ageing, and beginning to show signs of wear, so I had had a new one made, which fitted both dogs. Josse is much bigger round the chest than Chita is, and hers is too small for him.

He looked at her. Chita had that odd thing on, so maybe it was all right. I didn't track at all that first day. I let him walk around in the harness until he forgot it was on.

Next time we went to Maes y Porth I picked the biggest field and laid Chita's track first. I had only entered two Trials that year, as most were too far away, and I didn't want to kennel Josse more than I had to. One Trial would in any case show me what I needed to know. Chita's first Trial that year had been disastrous as we had had the track fouled by a stray puppy that played all around the field. That completely unsettled her.

The second was in a few weeks' time. Josse was to stay at Callanway again, as I still doubted if he would behave in a hotel. I wasn't staying at the Ellesmere where Angela would have let me eat in my room, and not leave the dogs. This Trial was in Shropshire, not Cheshire. He had not yet stopped crying when I went out of his sight in strange places.

Meanwhile Josse could start to track.

It was no use whatever using any toy, as there was nothing he wanted to pick up. He would run if a ball was thrown, and look at it. Balls had obviously never been part of his life. The quoit held no interest for him. He watched Chita swank around with her huge sticks, but he had no urge to copy her.

Running free, he investigated the grass, intent on bird smells. Birds fascinated him. He was still likely to chase if he saw a bird on the field in the distance, and it flew. He never did catch them, but that was to change when the next spring came around and Josse brought me three baby birds, all unable to fly. He carried them gently, and handed them over to me unharmed, expecting to be praised.

I haven't solved that, as I can't scold him. If I did he would think it wrong to bring me the bird. As I have never seen him catch it, it is better to have it brought unharmed than to have him take it off, and perhaps be triggered by its movements to kill it. One did die of shock. The other two I put in the hedge and their parents fed them, and both are now flying around the place, though very careful to stay well clear of dogs.

The birds now make the same alarm calls when they see the dogs as they do when the cats are about. They never did that before Josse came.

I laid Josse a short track at the opposite end of the field from Chita's track. I put a slice of brown bread at the end of it as he is as hooked on that as Chita. They often try to lead me to the breadbin during the day, even though they know perfectly well they only get it at certain times. Dogs know that humans are inconsistent and that it's always worth a try.

Once, just before he died, Janus barked in the night. I thought he wanted to go out, but he led me to the breadbin. Maybe he had been dreaming of bread. He didn't get it, or I would have been summoned every night after that.

That first track was only ten yards long. Josse had seen me put down the bread, and raced towards it. The second track was fifty yards long, as the dog knew what he was doing. He put his nose down, and he went. He went far too fast for my liking. He pulled ahead on his forty-foot line, and it took all my strength to hold him.

I had to lean back against the line, and even then he was hard to follow. I didn't want to check him at that stage. It could have put him right off.

A moment later he was even harder to hold.

A pheasant flew up from the long grass.

Josse lunged, tearing the line out of my hands so that it left burns, which were painful for days afterwards. The end snaked round my ankles and felled me. I went headlong, face down in wet grass with both hands in a muddy puddle where cattle had trodden the week before. Luckily the end pulled free, or I would have been dragged.

I picked myself up, cursing my dog. He was well down the field, racing at top speed, his mind focused on the bird in the air just ahead of him. The field was secure and he couldn't get through the hedge, which was strengthened with wire to keep cattle and sheep in. They took it in turns to graze there. The bird flew over the hedge.

Josse heard my calls at last and came back, full of glee. He had had a tremendous chase and it had been great fun. There was no point in finishing the track, as I had been dragged across it and he had run beside it.

I would have to work out a way to stop him bird-hunting. I would have to put him back on the long-line and teach him to come when called – every time, not just when he chose. I would have to make him drop on command, always, as Chita now did, not just sometimes. I would have to work out a way to slow him down when tracking, so that I could actually hold him. I had visions of racing round the tracking field, out of control, as my dog sped to his goal. That does happen with some dogs. Not all are trained to top standard, and the young ones have to learn by experience. They never start fully trained.

Josse's next track was on our own land, laid uphill. That does slow him down, but even so, he is more enthusiastic than Chita, and works quite differently. If he loses the line, where the tracklayer has turned a corner, he searches carefully. She used to panic until she learned that the tracklayer hadn't taken flight, but merely changed direction.

Early tracks are laid with very short steps, and when the corner is turned, as one walks normally, and doesn't put down any kind of scent other than that from one's shoes, then the ground is well stamped so that the dog finds plenty of scent

56

there and learning is easy. Josse had far more help on his tracks than Chita, who now had to follow where someone had walked as if out on a normal walk, with no extra clues left for her.

It was fascinating to train both dogs, as their style was so different.

Then came the day of Chita's second Trials.

We were on a helicopter station, where the grass was short, and the airfield stretched for what seemed like miles in every direction. It was a wonderful venue. It was also a wonderful day, a small breeze blowing, blue sky, and warm. Chita and I had to track in the early afternoon.

I took her out, put her harness on and reached the first post. There was a second thirty yards away, in a straight line, showing our initial direction. After that we might go anywhere. Chita was dancing with impatience; the judge was waiting, his scorepad at the ready; and we were off.

Our early Trials had usually resorted in abortive tracks, with all kinds of things going wrong. Since about thirty dogs enter every stake, and only five or six qualify, we didn't feel defeated. One needed luck as well as skill. Skill couldn't eliminate a failure caused by a stray dog blotting out all the track, or unseen hikers walking over it, only moments before the tracklayer arrived to walk there. Nobody stands guard over the fields beforehand, and anything may happen. Farmers usually tell the Trials management if they are going to spray a field, but it has been known for a farm-hand who was unaware of the Trials going on, to come and start spraying after a track has been laid. Since it is hard to find land for a half-mile track for each of sixty or more dogs, that is a major disaster. It's a worse disaster if it's done the evening before and nobody knows, as the spray harms the dogs, who inhale it from the ground.

There are other hazards too, due to the fact that no one knows the fields well. One of our tracks in Chita's early days led to a badger sett, or rather Chita led me there, the track went elsewhere. So I was prepared for anything.

I was not prepared for the heady excitement of seeing my little bitch put her nose down, and set off, working like an experienced dog, oblivious to everything. It goes here . . . and here, and it turns here, and we go here, and there's another turn.

57

She was pulling for all she was worth, but being much smaller than Josse, and half his weight, I could hold her. I had lost all sense of direction. We had already turned at ninety degrees twice, and then we turned a third time, this time at a much sharper angle, and went back on our tracks. She had to be wrong. I thought she had come back on a leg she had already worked, and was repeating herself.

She nosed the ground. Hare droppings. Maybe she wasn't backtracking, but had picked up a scent that ran alongside the part of the track she had already worked out. I was sure we were following a hare's line. She'd done that before, as had many another dog. 'Chita, track.' She left the droppings, and put her nose down about two feet away and hurried on. She was tracking something. We turned towards the judge for about eighty yards, and I thought we must have come to the end. It was only a half-mile track. We seemed to have been out there on our own for ever.

She turned away, leaving the judge behind us again. We were going right out into the country, miles from anywhere and she was going with such determination that she had to be following some positive line. She certainly wasn't just going for a walk. Maybe somebody else had walked that way before the track was laid. I knew the judge was now well behind me, and I had expected the end of the track to be near him.

We went on, and on and on. I knew we were wrong. Another track blown. All that work wasted.

Chita stopped and put her head down, and turned and looked at me.

I ran up to her.

There, on the ground, was a piece of wood, about six inches long, painted white, on which were the words 'WELL DONE'.

I couldn't believe it. I had her rubber cylinder in my pocket and threw it for her after I had taken her harness off, and she raced after it, and raced back. 'Did it. Did it. Did it,' her body said, ecstatic, sensing my feeling of terrific achievement, sensing that I was delighted with her. She raced to the judge and barked at him, and he laughed at her.

'What a dog!' he said. Most Obedience people had hated Chita; she had too much life in her for their routines. They need far more biddable dogs. Trials people, if experienced, always loved her, and envied me. She was so much more fun than a dog that learned reluctantly, as I was discovering with Josse. He was difficult to motivate. She, so long as she was able to work independently, was now very easy indeed.

'She did that beautifully,' the judge said.

The hours spent tracking had paid off. Chita had excelled herself.

We'd scored 104/110. She had cut one corner, and I, not believing her, had almost prevented her from following the right line; that cost us two marks each. The last two were lost for the time she spent sniffing hare droppings.

She found three articles out of the four in her search; she only needed to find two to qualify. She had full marks for agility. Her heelwork and sendaway, running out a hundred yards towards a windsock, were not perfect but she didn't disgrace herself. Then came the final test. The downstay, which Chita loathes, due to that long ago fight beside her.

I had practised and practised and she never broke at home, nor at Eric's, nor in club.

We had to hide behind a bunker, twenty feet from the dogs. We had to climb over it, not round it, which was not easy. Lying against the damp sandy bank, I held my breath. Ten minutes feels like a century. Would Chita stay?

One minute. Two minutes. Three minutes. Four minutes. Five minutes. Six minutes. That seconds hand on my watch crept round. Seven minutes. A small nose burrowed into my neck. A small apologetic body crept down the sand and into my arms. 'Can't take it. Not when you go. Not with dogs I don't know. Might fight,' her body said. A moment later another bitch joined her owner.

It was another 'if only' day. If only she'd stayed, we'd have qualified and gained those much sought after letters after her name. U.D.Ex. Utility Dog, excellent.

There was always next year. Or was there? Chita would be nine. And that scale was getting difficult. She no longer flew over. Some days it was a bit of a struggle. She had been lame during the winter, briefly, with a twinge of arthritis in her hips.

She has one last chance. One more Trial this year, and that's the end of our Trialling, as everything else is three or four hundred miles away. By the time they start next year, late in March, Chita will be going on ten; and even Chita may not be able to continue jumping at that age. There are not nearly so many Trials as there are Obedience Shows, as so much land is needed and there are none in the summer months, when the fields are under crops. They usually start again after harvest.

So it is up to Josse. And he is a very unknown quantity, as, if he doesn't get over his fear of strange places, it isn't worth trying. It would be cruel to the dog.

That fear has to be conquered so that it vanishes entirely.

Even now, as I write, after owning him for more than a year, it is still with him, and though I rarely see it in the places he knows, it is as strong as ever if we come to somewhere entirely new to him.

Nobody knows what the years ahead will bring.

Chapter Nine

The early months with any new dog, whether it has had a home beforehand or not, are tiresome months in some ways. The animal has so much to learn. I had a frantic phone call the other day from a new owner of a first-time pup. They had bought it at seven weeks old which is too young to leave its mother. It needs that extra week of parental discipline and living with a litter so that it learns how to relate to other dogs.

A week is a long time in a pup's life.

The caller had never had a dog before and had advice from a number of people well steeped in old wives' tales. The poor baby puddled and messed, and had his nose rubbed in it and was smacked. At seven weeks he has no control whatever over his bowels or bladder, and won't have for some time. I told her how to paper-train him while so tiny, as he won't be clean at night for weeks.

Paper all over the floor at first, so he can use it and associate it with relieving himself acceptably, and then paper on half the floor; and then on a quarter of the floor, and then only by the back door. By about eighteen weeks the paper should be removed for most dogs, but there is always the odd one with a weakness, that may need it longer. Human babies aren't house-trained at the same age!

I told her how to lift him gently, hands securely supporting his rump and his chest, cuddling him tightly, not grabbing him round the tummy. I told her how to take him out, every hour, after every feed, every time he wakes up, and before playing with him. I told her she needed to stay with him when out, as he would otherwise not know why he was sent outside and be sure it was a punishment, depriving him of company.

Tense and frightened, alone in the big world without any reassurance if something happens to scare him even more, and at seven weeks old a great many things will be scary, he won't relax, he won't do anything. At last the owner thinks he has been out long enough, expecting him to know by some kind of magical intelligence why he is out there, and lets him in. He relaxes with delight. They want me again, and it all happens as he lets go of those tight muscles.

Outside, when he does perform in an acceptable place, he needs to be praised as if he had just presented his owner with the crown jewels. 'Good puppy. Clever puppy, that's what I want,' in a voice that makes him realise this is good, and he will do his best to earn that lovely warm voice again. So many tiny dogs endure hell while they are being house-trained.

It is lovely to see a pup when he is first praised for doing something right. In the early weeks everything has probably been, 'no, bad puppy,' without any relief for many dogs. He has been scolded for all of his life with the owner because he hasn't been shown what is right and wrong, till he first comes to club. Tell him to sit; show him how to sit. Now tell him what a good dog he is. The pup grows in stature. 'I'm clever. She likes me, after all. I've done something right,' and within a week or two, if the owner learns how to praise and when to praise, the pup changes his behaviour and does his best to earn his reward.

But until he has heard praise for the correct actions he can't learn; he doesn't know what is right and what is wrong and dogs have no code of conduct. They are opportunists and if food is left about they eat it, because that's what food is for. No use trying to explain the caviare and smoked salmon sandwiches you put out so enticingly were for your bridge friends, not your dog. He doesn't even know the bridge friends are coming.

Many people humanise their dogs. 'Bad dog, into the garage for two hours to make you realise you've done wrong.' He doesn't understand. OK, he's been shoved outside, so if he is sensible he'll go to sleep, knowing he isn't wanted but with no idea why.

Some owners keep up a running commentary, saying, 'you naughty dog, what did you do that for? You know you mustn't.' That doesn't tell him anything either. He needs to be caught in the act, shaken when he is doing wrong, and at no other time. An older dog will associate a mess with anger; he's seen anger before and been shown what he did wrong. Often it isn't his fault; some dogs are left alone for far too long and are unable to hang on.

It is easy to tell by a dog's attitude to you and his own actions, and your response to them, how he has been reared. The first thing that was very obvious with Josse is that nobody he ever lived with had been unkind to him. He shows no fear of lifted objects, of a lead held carelessly as if it might be going to be used to strike him, of a foot that treads on him accidentally. He doesn't need a loud voice, but he doesn't worry if someone does shout at him. Many people seem to think a dog can't hear anything lower than a yell, but dogs' hearing is much more sensitive than ours, and they can easily be trained in whispers.

So much depends on the type of dog. There are no hard and fast rules. Chita taught me that long ago, and has taught others, if they were teachable.

Josse accepts the word 'no' instantly, obeys it, and remembers. Chita might obey it this time; but if it is 'no you can't' to something she wants to do badly, next time she will try and get away with it. Bitches can be much more sly than dogs.

I have never been sure till now if she fails to understand, because I haven't explained properly or is just being plain awkward, going to do as she chooses, and blow me.

I know now that the latter is the right answer, as she and Josse receive the same commands, and mostly he obeys and she still doesn't, except on odd occasions when she surprises me. It suits her to obey me then. She'll be boss if she can get away with it and never ceases her challenge.

Every time the dogs go out of the door together into the garden, Chita turns on Josse and bullies him. He may run inside or run to me, or very occasionally turn on her. She has been told 'no' a thousand times; it makes no odds. If she sees I am near enough to get hold of her and correct her physically, she won't do it, but if the car is out of the garage, she runs round it, knowing I can't see her, or what she is planning, and hides until Josse comes out, and then pounces on him. She is expressing dominance and though she is top dog and her own need is to remind him, she goes beyond the limit on occasion.

63

I have been told not to correct this, but if she oversteps the bounds, which she can do in sheer excitement, as she is still apt to go to extremes, she could hurt him. He doesn't retaliate, even when provoked to extremes, by anything more than a bark at her. 'Leave me alone, you horrible bitch.' Many people fail to understand this and think she is an unpleasant animal, but she is simply exhibiting the characteristics of the queen of the kennels.

When we were away some months ago I took her for a walk by herself, while Josse stayed in the car. We met someone with a male Rottweiler stud dog.

'Walk with us,' the owner said. 'He'll enjoy her company. Let her off her lead.'

'She's apt to bully,' I said.

'Well of course. She's a bitch and he's a dog. She'll keep him in his place, subordinate to her. He won't worry. He's very experienced with bitches. He'll ignore her.'

He did, as Josse does, and within a few minutes she was bored with trying to make him react, and the pair ran together happily, nosing the same smells, chasing after each other, and she had a wonderful walk. Often other dog owners worry about her bossiness, and protect their own dogs. She settles once she's made her point and behaves normally. 'I'm boss – just you remember it.'

When we went training with a Trials group at Runcorn some years ago, we allowed our ten dogs to run together after the lesson for a few weeks, until the summer traffic became bad and the journey took too long.

They were carefully chosen, watched beforehand to make sure all got on well, and then allowed to run free together in an isolated place, well away from the roads. This was very good for all of them, and there was no trouble, except just once when a dog pestered Chita, who is spayed and has no desire to be provocative or flirty. She told him off, but did come when I called to her. I ran away fast and, being afraid I was abandoning her, she raced after me.

Dogs, like people, aren't friendly all the time, but fights rarely become serious unless humans intervene. Then the dog is protecting his owner and the attitude changes. If both owners stand well away and don't interfere, the majority of fights end before they start, with the dogs, honour satisfied, returning to their handlers.

Josse hates fights. He prefers a quiet life, and doesn't challenge, but not being a fool he will stand up for himself if necessary. It has been necessary twice, once when he was attacked on his first walk with me, which unfortunately put him off black Labradors, so that he threatened any he saw. Up to then he had not met an unpleasant dog and it changed his attitude to all dogs except Chita. Only recently has he accepted black Megan, who trains with us, and now they will play together, though rather warily.

The second time was infuriating. I had been taking Josse to Pentraeth to the dog club there on Tuesday evenings (when our club met on Thursdays), to get him used to other dogs. With that and the trip to Macclesfield to work in a group there, by constant watchfulness and checking, I had convinced him that he should not lunge and bark at every dog he saw.

It was a long slow process, taking many weeks.

He had come into our club at the end of the evening several times, when I wasn't too tired after teaching for three hours, and begun to behave normally.

Then, one sunny day, after I had had several lovely walks with him and he had not barked at any dog that passed us, so that I felt the problem was cured, I was line-training him in the garden. The partridges were nesting in the hedge and he was fascinated by that hedge. He ran along it, his nose buried in hawthorn, and would not come when called. It is the only time he disobeys as he is still bird crazy.

That morning he had run up the drive, smelt partridge, and found the fox gap, which I had forgotten about. He dived through a supposedly dogproof hedge, jumped the wire on the other side, and landed in the old sheepfield, which luckily has now been planted with carrots.

I raced out of the gate and up the lane and in at the next gate, to see Josse chasing madly round the field, with partridges flying in every direction.

One bird was running, dragging a leg, and I thought it

injured until I remembered their distraction technique. She was luring the dog as far away from her nest as possible.

He was having a wonderful game. There were about twenty birds, and as soon as he had chased one off, another was there. It took me a long worrying time to make him hear me, and then he came and greeted me with extreme pleasure, obviously telling me this was a lovely way to spend a morning.

I took him in, filled the gap in the hedge with weldmesh, and planned a lesson at lunchtime. I put on the long-line and as he raced at the hedge, back to the gap where the nest had been, I pulled on it, said, 'no, come,' and brought him to me, rewarding him when he came. The lesson was going splendidly, with Chita running around us, also sniffing the ground, but unbothered by partridges.

A neighbour walked down the lane with her Collie, off-lead. The Collie put his head through the gate and barked at Josse. Both my dogs ran. The line ripped out of my hands, breaking as it did so, leaving me with a painful blister right across each palm.

I shouted 'down' and Chita dropped as if she had been shot. Josse raced on, reached the gate and tried to get through it.

He jammed there. All hell broke loose.

The Collie attacked him, making the most of a captive victim. Josse's roars of fury deafened me. Neither dog would stop fighting, and just as I reached Josse, and caught the now very short piece of line, he managed to get through and chase the Collie off.

The Collie's owner followed, apologising profusely. I called Josse and he turned to come to me. The Collie, seeing my dog's back, raced in, and bit his tail. His owner managed to get hold of him and they vanished, and back came Josse, leaving a trail of blood behind him.

I had not yet had my lunch but I had no option but to ring the vet and go straight over to him. Josse had been bitten through the lips, the tongue, the inside of his cheeks. He had a long gash under his eye with the eyeball exposed. He had lost his dewclaw, and that was producing a copious flow of

66

blood. His tail had also been bitten. The other dog's owner rang up a few days later, and was astounded at the damage. Her dog hadn't a mark on him.

Josse had his bites treated, and behaved very well. He was extremely sore, and moved as if he ached all over. That night he found eating very painful, but he persisted, which was one good sign. I had returned from our vet, which is twelve miles away, to eat a very belated lunch at about three o'clock. Josse lay beside me and I watched his face swell up to about three times it's normal size.

I rang the vet and took him back and he had an injection. I had a very subdued dog for three days. All the bites healed except for the one by his eye. That has left a scar, so that the lower lid has a triangular slit in it, but he was very lucky that the eye itself had not been damaged.

The worst part of that episode was that Josse reverted completely and raved at every dog he met, and behaved as badly in club and at other training sessions as he had after the first fight. 'I'll kill you before you kill me.' It was plain panic reaction, a warning to the other dogs to keep away, please.

But it couldn't be allowed.

This is far from peculiar to Josse. Many dogs are aggressive with other dogs, maybe due to being attacked by a dog running free, and not under control or because the puppy has not been sufficiently exposed to dogs when young. The need to isolate them till after inoculations is harming many of them, and the guide dog people now instruct their puppy-walkers to take the puppies out and about before the inoculations are finished, as an antisocial guide dog is a worse disaster than the risk of a sick puppy.

Training Josse to accept other dogs was all to be gone through again, and even now he isn't entirely reliable when he meets a strange dog, and may still play me up in club if other dogs approach too closely.

It was, I thought, the worst setback I could have with him. I didn't know at that time that something much more harmful lay in wait for us.

There is now mesh over that gate. He can't get through again and no dog can stick its head through and bark at him.

67

The Collie walks down the lane early in the morning and late at night, at definite times, agreed with his owner, and I make sure my dogs are not out then. Let any other dog come down the lane, whether on-lead or off, and Josse goes berserk if he sees it.

He also barks at dogs on the pavement as we pass them in the car, which is aggravating, and had never happened before. It is very difficult indeed to cure, and although after some months he is much better, let him see a Collie walking along the pavement, and I have a crazy dog behind me.

Our next training sessions will have to be at sheepdog Trials where I can stand beside the car, and make him behave. I can do nothing while I am driving.

I suspect he hadn't been taken out and about much, as his behaviour in the car leaves a great deal to be desired, and I spend a lot of time thinking up new ways of making him be quiet. If I can make him lie down, which isn't easy as he knows that I can't enforce a command when I am driving, then all is peace, as he can't see out. Maybe a van would be better, but it is uncomfortable to drive on long journeys and I don't like so much blind area.

Chapter Ten

Although Josse had plainly never met cruel humans, he hadn't had a lot of training for living. There were all kinds of little things one didn't need to tell an adult dog that had lived with you for some years, that he didn't know about at all. Also it was necessary to handle him for months as if he were a puppy, with lots more praise than is normal for a trained dog, even in all the little things.

'Yes, you go to your bed now, while I do this, that's a good boy.' This surprised Chita, who knew she went to her bed on those occasions.

Josse cried like a puppy when he was left at night when he first came indoors, although he had learned not to cry in his kennel. I had heard him several times, and then he was quiet, but my neighbour complained that the dog kept up a yapping all night. I lay awake and listened. Yes, she was right. I went outside, and crept over to the kennel. Not a sound, but the yapping continued from the next field.

When he came in to sleep indoors, and realised I was leaving him alone, as Chita didn't rate as highly as I did as company, the crying began again. He had to be taught not to. It was some time before he was secure enough not to cry for me if I left the room, and he still, on occasion, reverts, so that as I go out of sight with Chita, away from the car, a long forlorn howl follows us. He howls if I leave him – even for a few minutes – in a strange house, with someone he has only just met. I represent security. No one else does.

He learned within about a week that we didn't like singing at night, and was quiet, as we knocked on the floor and shouted 'Quiet'. He was used to that at Eric's, where the dogs are kennelled underneath the sitting-room, in an old farmhouse that was built above the cow byres long ago.

Seveal times I woke to hear a shrill yap, and crept

downstairs. Not a sound from my dogs. The mystery was explained when our new neighbours moved into the house next door which had been empty for two years. A vixen and her cubs had made a home in their barn, which is in the next field. The foxes are still around and on occasion raid our bin, tipping it on its side and emptying everything all over the lawn, much to the dogs' interest next morning. If I remember I put pepper inside, to keep them off, but then I forget and it starts again.

I had to remember his insecurity and though I didn't pander to it, I did have to make allowances for it and reassure him all the time, so that extra praise was necessary. That also became necessary for Chita. 'Why tell him he's good, and not me?' By the time the dog is adult one doesn't need to praise for most things, but this dog did need it, as my rules were new to him. He was very easy to house-train as, being an adult dog, he could hold on, and once he realised that I was delighted when he performed in the right part of the garden, he went there instinctively. That took half a day. Indoors, no. Outdoors, yes. I didn't realise how fast he did learn, or he could have come indoors much sooner.

Other things weren't so easy to teach, and as soon as stress intervened, I had to stop teaching. At first, those stress symptoms came so quickly, after only a few minutes, or if he made a mistake and I checked him as I would have checked Chita, forgetting that though he was a big dog, he hadn't been my dog all his life, and he had been reared under different rules.

I didn't know those rules.

As he relaxed over the months, and gave me his loyalty as well as his affection, he proved to be a very different character from Chita in so many ways.

Chita endures grooming. She knows it has to be done, and she stands stoically, and I may have to hold her collar, or she will walk away.

'All right, if I must, but I don't know why I have to put up with it.' She endures stroking; she has never asked for it, till some months after Josse came. As a pup she squirmed to be free, loathed being picked up and, as a tiny pup, would bite if picked up. 'Put me down. I want to explore.'

70

Life was all 'I want' with Chita. Moreover, it was 'I want it now. Can't wait. Won't wait,' except that she house-trained within days, and was always an extremely clean little animal.

Her impatience was probably a help here as she would rush to the door and yell. 'Must go out. Now, quick.' Or she would commute in an agitated manner between me and the door, fixing me with her eyes, willing me to understand what she needed. In her early days, she did have a weak bladder, which she has tended to have all her life; she needed to go out so much more often than Janus and Puma, and I thought at first she was playing up just to get outside.

I soon learned she wasn't!

She learned over the years that she couldn't always have her own way; that she couldn't chase cats, or fight other dogs, or race after chickens or cattle or goats. She couldn't chew up my property; she had to behave in the car and not rush from side to side, barking as I drove.

Those teaching days were behind us. Now there was a new dog to teach. A new dog to learn about, and to try and pick up clues to his character in the way he behaved.

Josse adores being groomed. When I pick up the brush he races to me and presses against me, moaning with anticipation. Each grooming session is a delight to him, and he turns from one side to another, then rolls over, then stands up, without any commands at all. Chita still has to have those commands.

He groans with joy, and nibbles my hands and leans against me. He would prolong the pleasure for ever, and as I finish and go to put the brush and comb away again, he runs after me, pushes against me, nudges my hand. 'Do it again. Please.'

He loves being stroked. He leans against the stroker, eyes half closed in ecstacy. Nothing is more wonderful to Josse than hands on his body, petting and fussing him. He climbs into laps, knowing that all of him is too big, but we can have his top half, which is the important half, or he will lie on the settee, top half only ('not on the settee, am I? Tail's on the ground!') and paw at a hand. 'Come on, pet me. I need you to love me. I need to be wanted.'

Teaching him to come to me was easy, as I knelt when he arrived and fussed him. Fussing is a delight to Josse. He is an extremely affectionate dog. Visitors can endear themselves to him for ever by taking notice of him and letting him lean against them while a hand caresses his chest.

If Chita comes, bright-eyed, prick-eared, and noses me, and then sits in front of me and stares at me, she doesn't want petting. She wants brown bread. People have no value in her eyes except as providers and comforters if she feels ill or has damaged herself.

She does need me badly if she is ill. Recently she had to have an operation for her anal problems, which are a hazard with German Shepherds, due, some say, to their tail-set, which clamps the tail firmly against the dog's end, and doesn't allow air to penetrate as it does with most breeds.

Diseased internal tissue had to be cut away. Chita, recovering, needed me. She needed cuddling; she lay at my feet; she climbed into my lap. She was amazingly co-operative though in a great deal of pain, and so unlike herself in her need for affection that it was extremely noticeable. This unfortunately meant we had to cancel her last Trials this year.

Came the day she felt better, and she was off on her own ploys, coming briefly but no longer in urgent need of my comforting hands. 'More interesting things to do than stand and be fussed.'

Josse is interested in people. They fascinate him, and he sits in a rather absurd straddled position, almost a puppy-sit, his eyes going from one face to another, from one movement to another, observing all the time. He associates two things much more quickly than Chita, who sometimes never makes an association and often makes the wrong one, by jumping to conclusions too early.

She reminds me of the type of quick-thinking person who is so impatient that he or she finishes your sentences for you, frequently finishing them quite wrongly, as they haven't been listening properly to what you are saying.

Josse is much more patient. He waits to see what the next move is going to be. If I pick up the dog bowls it may be to wash them. Chita 'knows' she is going to get more food.

Josse during his first week with us – unhappy, bewildered, unsettled.

Josse and Chita. Under control and paying attention. What are we going to do next?

Two dogs together are never easy to control. Josse and Chita practising off-lead heeling under control.

Agility practice – a lovely leap over the hurdle by Chita, an experienced dog.

Fonz to the attack. This type of work was new to Liz.

Chita's bugbear: staying still. Here she can't rebel – on the lead she is under control.

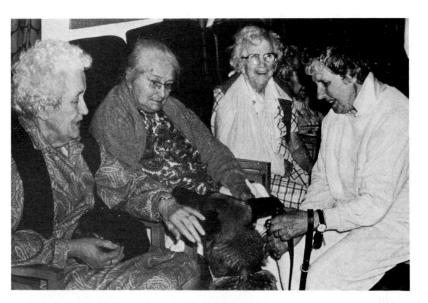

Above: Chita at Ysbytty Gwynedd on a PAT dog visit.

Left: David Morgan and Gretal walking together.

Fascinated course members and their dogs watch the sheepdog demonstration.

We work on the courses in all weathers, well protected against rain.

Demonstrating dumb-bell training on the first 'Course with a Difference'.

Josse – he's our dog now and a very happy dog.

Bowl means food, even if it is the wrong time. Even if in all of her life she has never been fed at that particular time. I may have forgotten to pick the bowls up and put them away. She puts on her 'going to get my dinner act', dancing and twisting on the spot, squealing with anticipation. When the bowl is put in the sink and the tap turned on, or it is put away in the cupboard, instead of being filled with her dinner, she droops, utterly disconsolate, and goes away, disappointed. Wrong again.

Josse watches more carefully. What is she going to do next? He is as hopeful as Chita that he might be mistaken but he knows it isn't feeding time, and as the bowls go into the sink he sighs and goes to bed. Just as I thought. No food now.

I thought at first his reaction was wariness, an anxiety not to transgress, in case I too decided I didn't want him, if a dog can think that way. It probably can't, but I was quite positive by now that Josse associated his lead, the car, and a strange house with a possibility of being dumped yet again. The three things together still caused him to cry, and refuse to come out of the car.

That fear overrides fear of other dogs, and he will ignore them and concentrate on me in a place that is completely new to him.

After more than a year this still triggers fear, but that is now the only time that he is really worried, and difficult to reassure. The only thing to do is put him back in the car and let him stay there, even if Chita comes in visiting.

He learns very fast and is often very funny. Chita has known for years that pea-picking time is wonderful, as we pod peas galore and freeze them and some of them always fly out of the shells onto the floor. She associates large bowls of peas with pleasure.

The first time we did this in Josse's presence he regarded everything with extreme suspicion. What on earth are they doing now? Honestly, humans! One of the peas shot in his direction, Chita dived for it but Josse got there first. If she wanted it, it had to be good. It was good.

His eyes lit up with anticipation and he pushed Chita away from my side and sat there himself, watching every pod. 'Please drop one, do,' those eyes said. He now adores peas, and also,

73

surprisingly, proved to adore blackcurrants and gooseberries if they dropped on the floor. Chita had never tried fruit, but if Josse could eat it so could she, and she grabbed too if a berry fell.

'Gooseberries. Ugh.' She made a face as she ate them, but if she didn't eat them Josse would and she wasn't having that. She'd suffer the sour taste rather than let him have more than his share.

One afternoon soon after he came indoors for good I fetched an apple and began to peel it. Josse had been asleep on the rug, but he sat up and stared at me. He raced at me, and pawed my hand. I stared back. What on earth did the dog want? I was too slow, too stupid to understand, and, very gently, he eased my hand away from the plate and removed the apple peel. I gave him the second piece and was rewarded with a Josse dance. Chita's dance is to circle fast on the spot, on her hind legs, like a Collie, filled with impatience but knowing she mustn't race around.

Josse does a little stamping ceremony on all four paws, reminding me of Janus who did something similar. Beat beat, beat, on the spot, his tail waving wildly, and then he nudges my hand hard. It was only too obvious that his first owner had shared apple peel with him. It didn't take long for Chita to learn that too, as she wasn't going to be outdone, or miss out on a possible source of food. Now both dogs sit expectantly, watching my hands as they peel, and wait to have the trophy shared between them.

Pear skin was even better. Once they had had that they became choosy about the apples and if I make a mistake and bring home tasteless ones, both spit out the peel and look at me in disgust.

They both enjoy all kinds of foods added to their basic diet. Lettuce and parsley to stave off Chita's arthritis, both well chopped. Carrots and broad beans, cauliflower and beetroot. If there is chicken soup to moisten their dinner, they are in heaven, and eat with expressions of utter bliss that are very funny to watch. 'Cor, that was nice!'

Josse had to learn the hard way, and so did I, that all food was not for him. He had only been indoors for two days when I cooked a chicken, removed it from the oven and put it on a plate

74

to cool, as I wanted it cold with salad next day. The phone rang before I could put it in the refrigerator. Neither Chita nor Janus ever stole, and I had forgotten about thieving dogs, although Puma had been a terrific thief. But she had been gone for nearly five years.

When I returned there was a broken plate on the floor and nothing else. I thought Kenneth had put the chicken away, and went on with preparations for our meal. Josse spent an uncomfortable evening, roaming restlessly, and next day had a very upset tummy.

I still didn't realise why, until I looked for the chicken and couldn't find it. 'Where did you put the chicken?' I asked Kenneth.

'What chicken?'

I looked at my unhappy dog. His eyes were forlorn and he obviously had tummyache. He had eaten a whole four-pound bird, bones, and all, and what is more eaten it almost red hot, and in about five minutes. It also explained Chita's odd behaviour. She had been lying under the table, looking distinctly miserable, and approached me a number of times as if she had transgressed too, but I was pretty sure she had not been involved, as when Josse had chased the cat, Chita had shot under the table and glared at me in the same way. 'I'm not doing it. He is.'

'I'm a good dog.'

He came with me to the vet for examination. He had been lucky, as chicken bones can cause disaster, and perforate the dog's inside, being sharp. He recovered within three days, and reverted to his normal happy self. He is an extremely happy dog. Chita is often anxious, trying to understand things that are beyond her.

Josse was to steal just twice more before I caught him in the act and could make it plain to him by the displeasure in my voice that that was *my* food, not his. His second feast was on a tin of corned beef. I had just opened it, and, leaving it on the counter, turned to get a plate out of the cupboard and turned round again to see Josse vanishing with his trophy in his jaws. By the time I caught up with him it was all gone, and we had to have something else for sandwiches.

The third time was infuriating as it was Kenneth's birthday and I had bought avocado pear, which I'd put on a bed of lettuce, filled with prawns, and covered with a cocktail sauce that had taken an age to make. He did leave the lettuce behind, on both plates, which were ready to carry to the table. A pan boiled over and as I turned down the hotplate, Josse made the most of the fact that my back was turned to him and to our special treat.

The three episodes were several days apart, and each time I had forgotten his habit. Now I decided we would overcome it in a different way and instead of putting food away, I left it out, sat the dogs by the kitchen counter, the top of which is easy for Josse to reach, but not for Chita, and said 'no' over and over again.

Now, if I forget to move food when the phone rings, I can leave it, knowing Josse won't touch it. Nor will he touch our food if Kenneth takes it in to the room where we watch TV, and intend a lazy on-the-knees meal, and puts the tray on a table which is within reach of both dogs. He often forgets that dogs have odd habits, and are no more likely to be perfect than humans. If a nose comes near my plate, a sharp 'no, that's mine' drives off the would-be thief, and he or she lies down, eyes reproachful. 'You have three meals a day; we only have one. Not fair.'

As Josse settled in, he became more and more interesting. I soon realised that whereas Chita is extremely clever, she is not intelligent. Josse is intelligent.

One afternoon at Callanway my two dogs found a gap in the rail and post fence and went out on to the drive. I had been jumping them over Eric's apparatus. We called them back. Eric was with me and we watched them, fascinated. Josse, after three attempts to reach us, stood back, looked at the fence, and neatly jumped the second rail, as the gap under it was too narrow to squeeze through.

Chita didn't see him jump in, and became more and more agitated, trying to squeeze under first one part of the fence and then the other. I showed her how to jump, but she couldn't understand. In the end I had to go out to the top of the field to the gate and call her up there. She never did find out how Josse managed to get through the obstacle while she didn't.

She only panics now in new situations, as experience mostly has shown her how to behave when faced with familiar problems. Josse doesn't panic over that kind of problem at all. His panic is due to his past and to being savagely attacked by another dog, and not to his nature. He must have come from very good breeding and been an extremely stable pup, as he now shows signs of becoming an exceptionally sensible dog.

What we will not know for some years is how those six early changes of owner have affected him mentally and whether he will ever overcome the fear of being abandoned yet again. I do know that the training not to bark at every dog he sees is paying off, but that too is a slow business, and I only hope he isn't attacked again, as next time I may not be able to effect a cure at all.

Which may make Trials an impossible dream.

Chapter Eleven

It takes time to adjust to any change in life. The change from having one dog that was used to living with us, and had been for a number of years, to including a newcomer not only unused to us but bewildered by constant change was a big one.

Josse complicated life in many ways.

It was not possible to walk both dogs together, and may never be possible, as Chita knows when I don't have my full attention on her and plays up. She does it in several ways. She may walk along sulking, her attitude saying, 'What's he here for?' She may lag behind, while he forges ahead. Or she may decide to pull back to the car. I can deal with all three of these, but it's simply not worth the energy.

In any case, both dogs need individual teaching, individual training, and individual attention.

Josse complicated life when we visited. While Chita came in, had a nose around to see what was there, and then settled down. Josse clung to the car. He might come in for a minute or so, but he didn't settle. There were times he couldn't come in with us at all, and one of those was when we were asked to take part in the Elinor chatshow on HTV.

Josse had only been with us for a few weeks when it was to be recorded, and there was no way I could expose him to that particular experience at that time. He would have been terrified.

The programme was to be based on the dog club, and since it was not easy to select just three people to come with me, I chose our three rescued dogs, now all settled in their new homes with their owners.

Each had a very different history, and each lived in very different surroundings. Cindy was an English Setter. She, and three Irish Setters had all been bought from one of the Breed Rescue societies. She was a miserable animal when they first got her, but now she is well behaved and sensible. Phyllis had trained her in club. Phyllis Morley runs the Setters, our local pub, with her husband Chris, so Cindy has to be used to people coming and going, many of them, to cars parking and driving out. She lives a very full life, having to behave herself with all kinds of people, with children and now with a new baby.

Alix had spent her first six months tied up and teased. She is a tiny German Shepherd bitch, smaller than Chita and not nearly so well muscled. She is sweet natured and very good with older children but she is now posing problems because she does not like toddlers, and her owners' new baby is ten months old, and may be in danger from the dog. They have to watch Alix all the time. Yet with older children and adults she is always beautifully behaved.

At the time of the TV show, the baby was as yet unborn. Alix lives in a lonely cottage, and does not mix with many dogs or with a great number of people.

Toby, our third dog, had a very bad start in life and landed in Helen's hands when he was a year old. He had been running free all day till she got him, a habit that has been hard to cure, as Toby is a born escaper. He had a knife wound and a broken pelvis when rescued, and he loathed people, and tried to bite anyone who came near. Helen was only thirteen when she first brought Toby to club.

Eight years later, he is a lovely little dog, a funny little Staffordshire bull terrier crossed with goodness knows what.

Lastly there was Chita, who though bought as a pup had to be persuaded that her role in life was to be acceptable to people, and not to attack them and their dogs. She has working dogs in her ancestry, among them the sire of some very successful police dogs.

The producer and his secretary came to club to see us, and to watch the dogs being put through their paces. They nearly went off with our newest recruit, a tiny fifteen-week-old West Highland terrier named Janie, who adored everybody and especially loved being fussed and made much of.

We were to be pre-recorded, and we did not realise that the recording was to be made in front of a live audience of four hundred people, or that it was to be forty minutes long. We agonised over clothes to wear, but since nobody quite knew what to wear, and no one owned anything very fancy, we decided on our everyday clothes – to look as smart as possible, but not to dress up, as it is very difficult to work with a dog in dressy gear.

I had warned the TV presenters that we were not going to put on a circus act; Chita could have done quite a bit, but the set was tiny and in the end we had to adapt our performance completely, as there was no room for the dogs to move freely.

We spent the afternoon rehearsing, which was worrying, as the dogs rapidly became bored and switched off. Dogs need short spells of activity and can't take long spells. They would all be sleepy by the time our performance began.

It would have been much easier if they had been left out of the afternoon work, which was mostly conversation about dogs and dog clubs, about writing, and about the dogs we had with us. They were to jump a hurdle, but there wasn't room for the big dogs to take off or run on, so Toby did that. Chita and Alix could run through the tunnel, one going left to her handler and the other going right, and Cindy could do some heelwork. I could demonstrate the ways to show a dog how to sit, down, stand and come, on the spot. As it was, we rehearsed this part several times, the dogs becoming bored and less responsive. They would be able to rest from 5 pm to 7.30 pm.

Our clothes were taken from us to be pressed so that we would appear immaculate. I spent the afternoon and the evening meal time in a pair of enormous mens' trousers and an equally vast shirt, worrying in case my own clothes didn't turn up in my dressing-room. Chita wasn't at all sure she liked the very splendid dressing-room, and squealed every time I left her. She had her own rug on the floor.

Josse, outside in the car in the car-park, howled all the afternoon and most of the evening. After his walk, before our performance, I moved the car to the extreme end of the car-park, so that he couldn't be heard. I gave him a long walk, though it had to be round and round the enormous grass-edged car-park, but that didn't tire him. It did me!

The rehearsal went well except for one thing.

Elinor loves flowers, and her sets are always massed with them. There must have been forty boxes of them, all real, all gorgeous, and all, in that hot set, under the lights, giving off masses of pollen.

I have hay fever.

Within half an hour my eyes were streaming, my nose and throat were swelling and I began choking. By four o'clock they were making anxious noises about finding a doctor for me. Then Phyllis remembered that she had collected some antihistamine for her daughter who also had hay fever, but Kay couldn't take them as she was pregnant. Phyllis had them in her handbag to return.

The set was re-arranged, so that I could stand as far away from the flowers as possible, and some of the troughs were removed. I took the antihistamines, which did reduce the symptoms considerably, but even so I choked twice during the evening. The audience were very kind, and since the programme was to go out a couple of months later, that could be edited out.

The act before us, a very good one, consisted of dancing life-sized human 'puppets'; giant teddy bears in Victorian dress solemnly prancing about the stage. The dogs watched in astonishment, but accepted them as they passed and re-passed us, as they went on and off stage. Only Toby was upset by them, and growled and had to be removed to a distant corner.

We came on stage. Elinor told me about her own dog, a Collie she described as a lovable thug that attacks her fingers and her toes. We talked about dogs generally and I showed the audience how Chita will sit to any word anyone likes to call out! 'Mrs Thatcher', 'fish and chips', 'rhubarb', 'Neil Kinnock'. There were all kinds of suggestions and Chita obligingly sat each time I repeated the word, as we walked about the set.

She was actually watching my hands and feet, and not listening at all.

Toby was to hurdle. Even he, though small, had very little room. He looked at the hurdle. He looked at the audience. He looked at Helen. He had had enough of our silly games, and had been jumping that hurdle all afternoon. We knew he could do it. Why ask him again? He walked to it, walked nonchalantly underneath, turned round, sat down and looked at Helen.

'What are you going to do about that?'

There was a roar of laughter. Toby turned and looked at the audience. This was something he hadn't had before. Asked to repeat the exercise he performed with flair and waited for his applause. He got it.

Cindy walked on beautifully and as she is a very pretty bitch, she needed to do very little to gain her appreciation.

Then it was time for Chita and Alix. The tunnel was placed and Peter sent Alix through. She came out, and when he called her went straight to him and sat, gaining her applause. Chita, following close on Alix's heels, came out at a different angle and had to come to me, towards the audience. Alix had to go to the back of the set.

Chita suddenly saw all those people, a mass of faces, more than she had ever seen together in her life. She forgot me. She ran to the edge of the stage and stared at them. She simply couldn't believe there could be so many people.

There was a roar of laughter, and then she remembered. 'Supposed to be over there.' She came to me and sat, angelic dog, 'never do anything wrong do I,' and put her head on one side. She loved the wonderful noise the audience made. She's always played to the gallery. Janus did too.

When the show was ended and people began to stand up, someone in the front row spoke to her. Chita pulled me across the stage, off the stage and into the audience where she spent a wonderful twenty minutes being fussed and petted, while people asked questions about their own dogs.

It was only later in the dressing-room, collecting all our gear, ready to go home, that I realised how exhausting the day had been. A long drive and then several hours under those bright lights. Everyone had been made up except me, as I was allergic to the make-up they used and hadn't thought to bring my own. Nobody had ever made me up on other TV programmes as usually we were only on for five minutes at most.

Josse had given up crying for us and was lying disconsolately. He heard us coming and began to scrape desperately at the inside of the car door, trying to open it and come out. I gave him a quick walk and a fussing, before the long drive home from Mold, where we had been in the Theatr Clwyd, to Anglesey.

Our next TV appearance, also for HTV, was on the news programme when *Dog Days*, my last book, was published. This was easier as there was a studio interview without the dogs. Then back to the car-park to collect the cars and off to a big field by the beach, where I could show Chita's paces.

To my amazement when I reached the car-park my two dogs were racing around, hunting for me, watched by several men who were not prepared to try and catch them, and the car door was open. This mystified me, until an hour later, when Josse, seeing another dog, flipped his paw on to the inside handle, opened the door and leaped out. Luckily we were stationary at the time, filling up at the garage.

The car was immediately taken in to the garage to have the inside handle removed and to stop that little game. Josse might well have leaped out when I was doing sixty miles an hour.

Luckily both dogs had wanted me, had found my tracks near the studio entrance, but been unable to come in, and did not go off on their own. Had they done so they would have been in the middle of heavy traffic as we were just off the A5.

Chita this time was able to show off her paces with plenty of room, though it was a bitterly cold day with the wind nearly blowing my hair off, and her fur wind-streaked. When I saw the programme later I was pleased with her performance.

'Take Josse out,' they said.

I didn't think he would be up to it, but out he came, and began to walk beautifully. Just as they began to film him, someone came on to the field with her dog and let it off. This was more than Josse could stand. A dog racing about, doing as it chose while he was on the lead. He began to bark, wanting to join in.

We scrapped that effort. Josse would need a great deal more hard work on my part and a great deal more socialising with other dogs before he was able to perform in public.

The week after that there was a little dog show near us, and I took both dogs along. I showed Josse in one of the pedigree classes, as it was a show exempt from the usual Kennel Club rules and he could be shown although he has no papers to prove who he is.

I had to make up a name for him, and this proved extremely difficult. In the end I used the first two letters of five of my grandchildrens' names: Mairi, Morag, Jonathon, Jacob, Rebecca, and the last five letters of the sixth, Ruaraidh, and registered him on the active list, which means I can work in Trials with him, as Mamojojareraidh Josse, which is no odder a name than a great many others.

Chita's father is Elan von Michelstadter Rathaus of Dunmonaidh, a lovely dog, many of whose offspring have done very well in Working Trials. Some of his other daughters are smaller than Chita, so that accounts for her size, which is unusually small for a German Shepherd. Many of the German dogs that have been imported over the past few years have extremely long, complex names, so I had no problem with the one I chose for Josse.

He behaved very well.

He hadn't had the second fight then, and I had high hopes of soon having him up to standard, and maybe competing early in the next year with him, if not in Trials, then in the beginner Obedience classes.

It never does to make plans where dogs are concerned.

Chapter Twelve

I had had Josse about four months when Sean suggested a photography session. I often have letters from schoolchildren who are doing projects on my books, wanting photographs of my dogs, and though I have plenty of Chita, as yet I had none of Josse.

We didn't think photography in any public place would be a good idea, as we didn't want any on-lead pictures. It was no use trying to get off-lead pictures where other dogs or people were likely to appear, as he would either rush at the dogs, or race back to the car. We decided to try him at Sean's home, when I went over for lunch with them. If that failed, Sean would come over to us.

Sean's cottage is older than ours and far more interesting as it has not been added to, or if it has, the additions aren't obvious. The kitchen and bathroom are both modern. It is an old farmhouse, with barns and stables, at the end of a lane that terminates in a not very wide yard, with a deep ditch at the edge of it. Reversing is always a hazard, as the space is narrow and there is a danger of either going into the ditch or backing into Sean's or Tilda's cars, or the horse trailer. Reversing with Josse barking furiously at Sean and Tilda's two horses was even more daunting. I very cautiously did what felt like a ninety-nine-point turn instead of a three-point turn. It seemed safer.

It was the first time the Hagertys had met Josse. He came out of the car suspiciously, but I left the door to his cage wide open, and we didn't ask him to come into the house. That was impossible anyway as the house is ruled by their sealpoint Siamese cat, Barney, who is very definitely anti-dog. Barney was safely indoors, and had no desire whatever to come and investigate.

He is a very beautiful, very regal and extremely aloof cat,

who seldom deigns to favour visitors, though he will come out to see us when we visit for an evening meal. He will endure being stroked, but that is all. He appears to have a low opinion of the human race.

The two horses were fascinated by the dogs. Both intensely curious, they stood at the gate watching. Sue is chestnut. Freya appears to be a chameleon, and though she started grey seems to have changed colour, and is darker now. Josse hadn't, so far as I knew, met horses before, though he had met Donk and been taught that dogs don't bark at donkeys. He barked at the horses, and they skittered off, and stood heads down, wary, some distance away.

Chita meanwhile was busy exploring the garden. Josse joined her, but commuted between her and me, with one eye on the car. He got into it twice, and looked at me. OK, stay there. I didn't care, so long as he came out in the end. He needed to have his confidence. I didn't want photographs of an intensely worried dog. We had made sure we had plenty of time. All day, if need be. Photographic sessions with animals never can be hurried.

The door wasn't shut, the car was available, I didn't appear to be going to leave Josse behind and he began to relax. He came out again, checking frequently to make sure the door of the car remained open, made friends with Sean and Tilda, and then turned to explore the barn, which was well stocked with hay.

Sean now had the camera ready.

'Let's try a picture of the dogs with the horses,' Tilda suggested. The horses were back again, leaning on the gate, fascinated by all this odd activity. There was a scurry from the barn, and a loud mew of rage, and a cat appeared, racing up the lane. I called to Josse, and he returned, abandoning what had seemed to be an exciting chase.

He hadn't come to my call. There was something much more interesting beside the barn, crouching among the stacks.

A tiny kitten, not more than about five weeks old, crept out and stared at the dog. The dog stared back. I leashed him.

Up the lane the mother cat was almost demented. She was terrified of the dog and couldn't face him. She was terrified for her kitten, but couldn't bring herself to come back and fetch it.

She sat, wailing desperately, and we tried to shoo the kitten to her.

It was much too interested in what was happening beside the cottage. It had no fear of the dogs, even when Chita sniffed at it, and then turned to stare at me, her eyes asking what she was supposed to do about this tiny creature. She had never seen a cat so small.

It went to Tilda. It was a most attractive little animal, fluffy furred, round eyed, and totally fearless. It kept up a small rumbling purr, quite sure that all of us had the most friendly of intentions. Its mother by now was making so much noise that we were surprised the baby didn't run to her.

It did, at last, go half-way up the lane, and disappeared briefly among the stacks. The mother began to creep back, very slowly.

I put the dogs down by the gate in front of the horses, and Tilda had another bright idea. We would get the dogs looking at the horses and the horses looking at the dogs. If the four heads all looked at one another it would make a fascinating picture. That was asking a great deal.

I armed myself with dog biscuits and Tilda armed herself with apples, the theory being that horses loved apples and dogs loved dog biscuits. We ended by swopping titbits. My dogs were sure apples were nicer than biscuits and Sue and Freya were intrigued by the biscuits.

All the animals were now staring, not at the food, but at the ground behind Sean, where a very small, very determined, very tiny kitten was playing happily with a feather. The mother was now at the furthest edge of the barn, which runs lengthways at the side of the lane, crying louder than ever, a continuous wail of distress.

Tilda picked up the kitten and took it up the lane. Mother and kitten vanished fast. Josse and Chita had vanished fast too, Josse being back in the car, and Chita investigating the ground beyond the ditch, which appeared to smell wonderful. Her eyes were half-closed and she was sniffing dreamily. We called the dogs back, settled them both in a downstay angled to look at the horses, and took up our positions again, Tilda making inviting noises to Freya and Sue, and me making soothing noises to my dogs. I was rather glad we weren't anywhere public.

The camera clicked.

We looked at Freya. She had decided now was the time for all good horses to roar with laughter, and her face was twisted into the most extraordinary expression, her lips lifted, and all her teeth showing. Sue, disgusted, had turned her back. Chita was absolutely fascinated by Freya's curious antics, and Josse was creeping forward, apparently determined to reach Sean.

Who once more had the kitten between his feet.

It ran forwards, and stood between Josse's paws, staring up at him, apparently entranced by this enormous animal. He stared back at it in amazement. The mother cat's yells reached fever pitch. I had visions of one small cat being gobbled, and took hold of Josse's collar, though he was apparently too astounded to do more than stare. We would have loved a photograph but the grass was long and the kitten would have been invisible in the picture. We didn't dare keep it there.

This time Tilda picked it up and took it to the end of the lane, as near to the road as she dared. The mother cat belonged to the farm next door, where a number of cats lived in the barns, quite wild. No way would she come near people. As soon as Tilda was half-way down the lane, she seized her erring baby in her mouth and vanished, fast.

Tilda whistled to the horses, and once more Freya and Sue stood at the gate, staring down at the dogs this time. Josse behaved himself beautifully, keeping quite still, and suddenly the pose was perfect. Just as the camera was about to click, Freya swept her head down towards Josse, who leaped up and barked at her.

It took about ten minutes to settle dogs and horses again. It looked so good when they did co-operate that we were determined to go on trying. We were running out of titbits. Chita, who poses beautifully, was becoming restive. Josse, who had not met this sort of procedure before, was extremely hard to keep in one place. As he grew bolder he showed more and more of a desire to explore the haystacks, a desire which was explained when, releasing the dogs while Sean changed the film, he ran into the barn, barking, and a grey tom-cat exploded and dived through the fence. He must have been there all the time. He often visited, also coming from the farm and was probably the kitten's father.

Tilda was quite determined her idea should work. So back we went to stand with food in our hands and make funny noises at the four animals. Fortunately the weather was kind, and it was warm and still.

Whenever the horses were right, the dogs were wrong.

Chita discovered an itch under her tail and nibbled it fiercely just as the other three had settled very well. All four were right and again Sean was about to take the photograph when Josse stood, stretched, came to me, and filched the titbit from my hand.

At last we had what we wanted. We went, somewhat exhausted, to lunch, leaving the dogs in the car. In the afternoon we were to take Chita to Church Bay and photograph her by herself for the cover of *Dog Days*. That would be easy, after the morning session.

As usual we were wrong.

It was a lovely bright day and there were people on the beach and there were dogs on the beach. Several dogs. Dogs swimming, dogs barking, dogs racing after balls, dogs running around. We were on the cliffs above them, looking out to the further headland, to sandy stretches and to blue sea, with a cream of white round the base of the rocks.

Chita had already had one session of having to do as she was told. She hadn't been on these cliffs before. We had left Josse in the car in the car-park about five hundred yards away from us, in the village. We could hear him singing his misery. So could Chita. Every now and then she stopped and listened and came to nose me. Poor Josse. Why can't he come?

She found a rabbit scent and became deaf.

She decided her legs needed stretching and did a mad little race against her shadow, through the scrubby grass, vanishing behind minute bushes. She ran to the edge of the cliff and peered over. I called her. Several dogs had fallen on to the rocks below during the years I have been here. Janus, the year before he died, had chased after a seagull, and climbed a little rocky hummock and been stuck there, unable to reverse and come down. Rescuing him had been horrendous as he was a heavy dog, I was alone, the rocks were slippery and Chita had become demented, and tried to reach us both, so that I had had to leave him, leash her and tie her to a post that somebody had very conveniently stuck in the sand there, probably as part of some long ago outworks to stem the sea when it came in, or a relic of wartime beach defences that had been overlooked when they were removed.

I had no desire to have to scramble down these cliffs to rescue her.

At last we managed to calm Chita down and sit her. She looked gorgeous. Sean clicked the shutter just as a dog barked on the beach below. We have a splendid picture of her half crouched, tail in the air, back to the camera.

The antics of the dogs below us intrigued her and it was over an hour before we had the picture we needed.

Our last photograph of that series came a couple of weeks later when Sean was visiting us and, for the first time, Chita and Josse began to play as dogs should play, racing after one another, first one chasing the other and then reversing the roles. When they met they met with paws around one another, moaning with pleasure and licking one another's faces, though when the photograph was developed it looked rather more like an all-out fight!

Josse is due for another photographic session soon, as my mother has had to go into sheltered accommodation, and as I can't see her often, since she lives in Bexhill, which is more than three hundred miles from here, I send her pictures of us and our doings. My family all do that, so that at Christmas I often have as my present an album filled with photographs of our grandchildren throughout the year, which is lovely when we don't often meet.

Josse's next session ought to be easier as he now accepts commands and will sit and stay, and he has put on weight and lost the haunted look that was always in his eyes in any place new to him.

It's useless for me to try to photograph the dogs, because, as soon as I get them settled, they both come to nose my hands and try to find out exactly what I am doing. I can't concentrate on picture taking and on them at the same time, and don't they know it. My memories of Janus and Chia and Casey when small are of three animals playing together and as soon as I had the camera ready to immortalise them they all sat in a row and stared at it, or came to nose the lens. I missed so many gorgeous pictures!

Chapter Thirteen

So much of a dog's success as a pet depends on the dog itself, but also on the way it was reared in the nest. Those first eight weeks are critical. A pup brought up in a shed with only his mother and his litter mates, who doesn't see humans and isn't handled by them, will be as wary as a wild dog when he comes out into the world.

I met a litter like that some years ago in Ireland. The pups were twelve weeks old, and had been reared in a garden shed well away from the house. The bitch left them for her food, and nobody had been near them, owing to everyone being extremely busy.

I was asked to socialise them and the first thing I discovered, to my dismay, was that they had not even been outside the shed and their eyes couldn't stand the light. They were terrified of me and hid, and it took over a week to gain their trust. By the end of three weeks they did come out to play and they responded to me, but any other human approaching sent them into hiding again.

They were not at all satisfactory as either gundogs or pets when sold.

Another bitch, reared in isolation, this time a German Shepherd, has been at Callanway for months. Nobody can get near her. Now, after more than half a year, she will approach within yards of people, but never come up to them. She wears a long string on her collar so that the kennel girls can take hold of that to lead her back to the kennel after exercise.

Nobody bothered with her after she was born. She was left entirely to her own devices, and saw nothing of the world.

Another dog like her, rather younger and also a German Shepherd, has recently been rescued here. She remained with her parents, who were kept outside in a big kennel, and allowed the freedom of the farmyard. The dogs never go indoors and never leave the premises. No one takes much notice of them. They are guards, and that is all.

The little one, aged five months, was for sale, but so unresponsive to people, running from them, ears flat, eyes wild, that no one wanted her. Her new owner has a four-year-old very outgoing German Shepherd Dog, and he is helping bring his new companion out of her shell. She has come indoors, and trained easily to be clean, but she won't come near people, remaining very aloof and anxious, which is most undoglike.

Josse had none of that in him, but his training had to be to show him what the world was about, as he obviously hadn't been anywhere very much. Everything was new to him; everything was stressful, apart from the house, which was so plainly an environment he had once known well.

The six months he had spent in different kennels hadn't affected that initial background.

One of the most difficult things about any field of behaviour is that new research uncovers new facts all the time. What is considered well known in one generation is proved wrong in the next, because a frontier has been crossed, and a new mind brought to bear on the way we think about our animals.

I have always been told, and have read that pups ought to be sold around the eighth week, that younger pups lose much from an early sale, and older pups also lose out.

Yet in the issue of *Dog World*, dated 15 August 1986, Kay White, who is a well-known reporter on dog matters, writes about recent research carried out by Dr Tom Althaus, of the University of Berne.

Dr Althaus is concerned to see that there are fewer failures in dog/owner relationships, as the dog rescue homes in all countries are filled with pups bought in good faith, but turned out because they failed to be satisfactory pets. Often some other reason is given than this, as few owners will admit that they have failed to come to terms with a mere dog.

This lack of success can be due to the new home, but often it is due to the fact that comparatively few breeders know about the psychological needs of the puppies they rear.

The suggestion is that pups that are taught by their breeders are not sold until ten weeks old. This means they are easier to house-train as they now have bladder control, and some I have seen sold at twelve weeks have already been house-trained.

They sleep better, and aren't so easily scared. A little puppy has innumerable panics due to new situations and needs a great deal of reassurance. If he doesn't get it, then he becomes timid, or may bite in terror, not knowing any other way of making his feelings known.

According to Dr Althaus, the period from seven to nine weeks is a time of extreme sensitivity, during which the puppy can be terrified by all manner of strange situations. Few homes are so devoid of happenings that something can't go wrong. There are weird noises, inexplicable to a baby animal that can't understand that a washing machine can make a noise like a gun, sounding like a terrific thunderclap in those sensitive ears. Everything is impossible to understand.

He needs a great deal of sympathy at this stage, and often gets little, as people are convinced he understands the commands yelled at him, and can take anything that may happen in the house.

One of Janus's first nightmares was the windowcleaner suddenly appearing on his ladder at an upstairs window while I was making the beds. Luckily I had the pup with me. He had never seen a man hanging outside apparently in thin air and shot under the bed, trembling. I pulled him out, and took him downstairs and outside and called to Jim to come down the ladder and make friends with the dog.

Jim, having a dog himself, understood the situation, and after that Janus watched in amazement as he climbed the ladder to window after window, while I knelt with the dog in my arms, stroking and soothing him. Had I not done so, he might well have had a terror of windowcleaners for the rest of his life. Once he had seen the man, and ladder, and watched the man climb up and down he understood this was merely another peculiar human activity and not some sort of flyperson, able to hang in thin air.

A pup left on its own might well have this happen when nobody is there to reassure him. It is probably very difficult for humans to understand how it feels to be a midget in a giant world. If I have an insensitive handler in club I get him or her to lie on the floor and then have the tallest men loom over them, bend down over them with apparently threatening gestures and see if they can be made to understand how a tiny animal feels.

Very few people understand the power of the human voice. A couple of years ago I met a little vixen, who had been rescued when her mother was killed, and kept in a cage. She won't come near any human, I was told. I lay on the ground by the cage and talked to her. Everybody else stood well clear. After about half an hour she crept out, and within a few days I could stroke her, very gently, making careful movements through the bars of the cage.

Timid puppies react to that voice easily, looking up trustingly. A soothing croon. 'Good puppy. Good baby.'

It is the hardest thing in the world to get owners to talk to their animals. Once it was commonplace. Everyone knew that dogs and horses responded to a voice. How few people do know now came home vividly recently at a pony club meeting in an indoor riding school. One child failed to tie her young pony securely and he raced off, causing panic. The floor was hastily cleared and then a number of people, adults included, tried to head him off, making the panic far worse.

I stood by the rails and talked at him. Good baby. Come on baby, it's safe here – a constant soft stream of words that penetrated his frantic little brain. He came over to me. I gathered his reins and handed him back to his owner. As I did so I heard somebody say, 'Did you hear that bloody fool talking baby-talk to that pony?'

An older man, well versed in horse lore, was standing near me, and we exchanged a very eloquent glance of pity.

Dr Althaus's research brought so many memories to mind, and made me rethink what I had for so long imagined to be the correct procedure when selling a pup.

His suggestion is that selling time ought, ideally, to be either at six weeks old, before the fear period of seven to nine weeks starts, or after ten weeks. But Kay does end her article by saying, 'it must be emphasised that retaining pups until ten weeks and *not* educating them is the worst state of all.'

Thinking, more and more, about Josse, he gave me so many clues. He had been a well-reared puppy, for though he was thin when I got him as many adolescent animals are, he has good bone. His lack of confidence in new places is not due to his upbringing but to the frequent changes when he was about a year old. More and more, he shows that he was a very well-loved puppy for that first year, and that he was a housekept dog.

As he relaxed and grew used to us, and began, I think, to realise he was not going to be passed on yet again, he turned into one of the happiest animals I have owned.

Puma was an anxious dog, failing to understand the world around her, and not sure if she was doing right or wrong, needing constant reassurance. Janus was a clown, and his deafness made him difficult at times. He was extremely happy-go-lucky, a fool of a dog, but his merriment was not shared. It appeared when he had bettered a human, and won the day. Janus's sense of humour was all his own.

His affection was easily won with a titbit from anyone who chose to give it.

Chita is a much more complex character, and I suspect, without training, would have been an impossible one. She offers affection on her own terms, and will not take it when you choose, which is a sign of dominance. Call her for fussing because Josse is being fussed, and she will obey the call, and stand and look at you.

OK, baby him if you want to, but I have better things to do, and off she goes again. She may return and nose a hand, or put her paws on your knees, and stare at you. That doesn't mean she wants love. It means she wants brown bread, and is ordering you to get it for her. That ploy doesn't work, so she goes off to her bed, sighing deeply at the impossible ways of humans.

Josse was so different to all of them. Different to those other dogs of long ago: to Turk and Thor, to Brandy and Sheba, to the club dogs that have become part of my life, even though briefly.

Eric was right in that he is an easy dog. He is an extremely happy dog when not stressed, though only those who visit us become aware of that.

'I wouldn't have known it was the same dog,' club friends say when they came here for show committee meetings. Gone is all the worry, the desperate fear that someone may take his lead and take him away from me, that some dog may attack him. This is his home, his territory, where he can run with Chita, where he can search for wonderful scents on the ground, and where he is sure of the rules made for him, and knows how to behave.

Teaching at home was easy after a few months, and he forgot to rush off to the house or the car, when I started off-lead training so long as we were at home. Outside, he still might, and especially if I used the word 'Heel', which was obviously associated in his mind with rigid discipline.

I changed it to 'trit-trot', and within a few days had beautiful attentive heeling which he found great fun. Forget and say 'heel' and I lost my dog's confidence at once.

At the end of six months he could hurdle over three feet, scale six feet, and do a five-foot long jump, but had not learned how to extend himself to clear nine feet. His heeling was good, he loved short sendaways, and did not become confused over them as Chita had done. This was probably because I now knew what I was doing, and was sticking to one method, and not taking advice from people I thought knew better than I did. Their methods worked well for their dogs. Not for mine. I was using Eric's method, which is to play with the dog on the down spot, and then run back a few paces, run with him, put him down, praise and play again. The distance is gradually extended, and the dog learns to run out and lie down wherever he is told, in whatever direction you indicate.

Training Josse was much easier than training Chita in her early days because he wants to co-operate. She didn't. Away, I'd say, when I thought she was trained, and she'd give me an old-fashioned look and shoot away, in the opposite direction to that which I had indicated. Josse wanted to go where I wanted him, and the elation that comes when that happens is impossible to describe.

There was never a problem with calling Josse to me, so that exercise was easy.

97

Stays were not a problem at home, but anywhere else they are still an almost insuperable worry to him. It was months before he could bear me leaving him, in the park, or at the club, even if it was only two paces, and I held his lead. He crept to me and leaned against me. Don't leave me, please.

On the downstay he crawled to me and lay against my leg. It was weeks before I could move even two steps from him out of doors – anywhere but in our own garden. There I can leave the two dogs, go indoors, and come back again, and they won't have moved.

It will be a very long time indeed before I can do that with Josse anywhere but at home. It may never be possible. I dare not practise where other dogs are likely to appear and bark at him, as that would ruin all my work, and might trigger him to run and attack them. In summer, when everywhere is full of tourists, there are few places where I dare let the dogs run free. People can do unpredictable things and I don't know how Josse would react to a child who ran past him, yelling.

There is one place which has proved invaluable to me to further Josse's confidence and that is the Sea Zoo, where I took Chita to practise long downs among the chickens and geese.

These are now enclosed, but visible behind wire, and the zoo is so busy that in summer it has over fifty thousand visitors. It is a fascinating place, as all the exhibits come from the Menai Straits, in which there is an unbelievable variety of sea creatures.

There are two enormous car-parks, where cars come and go – and so do bicycles, motor cycles, motorised caravans, delivery trucks and lorries – and people are everywhere.

Men, women, children; people in wheelchairs, babies in buggies, babies slung to their mothers, children being carried pick-a-back. People eating ice-creams. Children racing about.

There are people carrying bags and boxes, people with packs on their backs, people with cameras and video cameras, all of which can bother a dog that has never seen such things before. It is a small, easily accessible area in which Josse could be exposed to new sights and crowds of people in a controlled environment. We know everybody there well, as David and his Labrador Haddock came to club for a year for Haddock to learn manners.

Chita did a great deal of her training there in the days before Josse came. It has the added advantage that I can shop there too, for fish straight out of the sea, and for unusual varieties such as skate, squid and monkfish, which are rarely found on sale here. This year they also sold particularly luscious strawberries.

We started going there several times a week early in the season when few people were about. Josse learned not to bark at cars parked next to us, or at people looking at him. Then he came outside and walked a little, at first – as always – stressed by his new surroundings. We played the 'in car, out of car' game, and then a little walk, past the geese, which triggered him to excitement. Sitstay watching the geese, with extreme difficulty, but he would stay for a few seconds, and after a few weeks I could walk him past the geese, say 'no' and he wouldn't even turn his head.

Downstay was a different matter. Not there with all those people about, and I haven't forced him. He now will go down in the park so long as nobody is about. If people are there, he is bothered. His eyes look haunted again, a very odd expression that rapidly betrays his feelings, and his ears go back, and he starts liplicking frantically.

He looks haunted in our extra room, which is built where there was once a very decrepit barn. That is where I have all my cat pictures: those from *Kym*, and several which I bought from Bill Geldart who illustrated *Kym*, or other cats he had owned. Cats all over the wall, everywhere. Josse stares at them and he becomes more and more anxious. He knows he mustn't chase Chia, though that knowledge still doesn't always prevent him. She fascinates him, and their meetings are very wary on her part, not trusting him at all. In this room he is surrounded by effigies of her. Even now, over a year later, he hasn't grown used to it, though he relaxes more quickly.

Oh, all those cats. Well, not real, are they, and I can take his mind off them. At first I couldn't. He walked around, head in air, looking. 'There's a cat, and another and another, and another. Cor!'

He will not stay down quietly in that room. He will now go down in club and lie quietly, watching while other dogs move about him, so long as they don't come too near. He can as yet only make contact with two of the bitches. Little German Shepherd Alix, smaller than Chita, makes friendly overtures which he accepts, and he will at last accept black Megan, who at first he refused to tolerate after he had been attacked by that black Labrador, running loose in the park the first day I had him. A very inauspicious beginning.

The other dogs frighten him, though only two have shown signs of aggression towards him. I am sure dogs, like children, sense fear, and as a result play on it, and bully the timid animal, enjoying the reaction they cause.

Chapter Fourteen

My really major problem has been teaching Josse to retrieve.

It was soon very obvious that playing with a ball had not been part of his life. He had no idea what to do with it, and if thrown, he didn't even bother to run after it, though it was rolling temptingly. He would watch Chita retrieving in amazement. Obviously he thought she was quite daft.

Eric had started a partial retrieve using a gundog dummy. The dog wasn't very interested, but would bring it a few feet. Never more. Offer him anything else to bring and he might run to it, nose it, and then flirt his tail and run off. Don't want that silly thing.

He much preferred bird-nesting, which became a nuisance, as there are nests everywhere in the hedge and he ran up and down it, startling the birds and infuriating them, so that the garden was noisy with their anger.

Try and get him to retrieve outside the back door, and I was instantly lost, as I always forgot the Hole. The Hole is in a tiny flower-bed that is based on rock. Nothing can be buried deep and the earth can't be dug. It contains berberis, potentillas, both yellow and red, and fuchsias, and in spring it is a mass of bulbs. Anything easy to grow and undemanding grows there as well as masses of wild pansies that get bigger every year, so that the once tiny flowers are now half the size of the big nursery-grown ones which I adore and have everywhere.

Throw anything here, and Josse ignores it and runs to the potentilla bush under which is the Hole, and noses it excitedly.

We were mystified for years by the Hole. It is round, and about two inches across. Fill it in and it re-appears. The grass round it has unusual qualities as the dogs sniff it ecstatically at night, unable to leave it and come in. Then, one winter when it was snowing hard, Kenneth called me to look out of the dining-room window.

There, beside the site of the Hole, was a weasel. He played with the snow, he somersaulted, and he scuffled it. He danced in the sunshine, alone, enraptured, enjoying life. It began to snow again, enormous flakes floating out of a nightblack sky, a sulphur glow on the distant horizon. He went to find his Hole, but it had been covered and vanished, and he changed from a relaxed happy little animal to one that was totally demented.

'It's gone. No home. Where's my hole?' He dug frantically in the wrong place. He scrabbled under our closed back door. He tried to get down the hole in the board that covers the drain to keep dead leaves out of it. Then, running along the flower-bed, one paw went downwards, into his front door, and with a frantic twist of his body, he was gone.

We saw him sometimes after that on a sunny day, basking, but the second anyone moves he vanishes. Josse, asked to retrieve there, much preferred to go weasel-hunting. He always tells me when we have had a nocturnal visitor, and he is much more interested in the evidence of the scent on the ground than Chita, who sniffs around, but not with Josse's total dedication.

He is a connoisseur of scent, savouring it, analysing it, obsessed by it. She sniffs and leaves it, and goes on to find something elsewhere. Maybe after nearly nine years on earth a dog grows blasé. At not quite three years old, everything is still to learn, and for Josse's first years he had perhaps been deprived of country living and was as innocent as a puppy. The only firm base I have for him is the RSPCA kennels at Rochdale which indicates that he started life in that area, which is industrial and very built-up.

I wanted him to retrieve, not only with competition perhaps one day in mind, but because it's fun for dog and owner.

The retrieve is the exercise that bonds dog and owner; it is co-operation, as opposed to dominating the dog. 'I said heel, so you heel, I said down, so you down.' It's no use trying to make a dog that won't retrieve retrieve the proper way at first. It doesn't know what you want at all.

There are ways of forcing a dog to retrieve but I don't like them. I'd rather have a dog that did it of his own free will, every time.

Josse was odd when it came to picking things up in his mouth. He simply froze and looked at me, terrified. I made a puppy toy from a pair of old socks, rolled up and stitched into a ball. I tried to make him take them in his mouth.

He spat them out. 'Ugh. What on earth are you doing?'

Chita swanked with her tree branches. He watched her, and then went bird-hunting in the grass. There is plenty of scope for this as magpies, pheasants, and partridges all spend a lot of time parading on our ground. The drive is always littered with snail shells, thrown down by the thrushes, and many other birds seem to root for worms. The dogs have persuaded next door's chickens it is wiser not to trespass. There is nothing quite so startling as seeing a screeching hen take off fast in front of a running dog, deaf to call commands. Luckily the hedges are not henproof though they are dog-proof. The hens can escape. The new ones always trespass. Puma once came back to me with two tail feathers in her mouth from a cock that hadn't been fast enough on the ground.

Since the grass is long and the birds are hidden I never see them, so I can't call the dogs off before the chase begins. I suppose I could keep the dogs penned, but it is our land. I began to check for chickens and all other forms of distraction before trying to get Josse to retrieve.

I did have some success with a gundog dummy, which is made of green canvas, stuffed to the weight of a hare. It is a long sausage-shaped object, that can be dragged or hurled for the dog to retrieve. Throw it a few feet and Josse would pick it up, walk a few steps and then drop it again.

I suspected as a puppy he had often been told to 'drop it'. I don't do that when my pups pick something up. I say, 'Clever pup. Let's have it then. What have you got? Aren't you lucky?' and the dog comes to me intrigued by my voice, and gives me his trophy.

I tried throwing things for Josse. He ran to them, nosed them, and ran off. Not interested.

I tried throwing something for both dogs. Chita raced out, Josse followed her, looked at her, said, 'It's all yours,' and trotted off again.

I tried dragging the dummy by a string to excite him. It didn't.

I tried kicking it, throwing it, tossing it. He just stared.

I tried putting it in his mouth and he panicked, so that was no good.

Then, one afternoon, I had done a search practice with Chita, hiding four articles in the long grass for her to find. A piece of wood about six inches long, a cartridge case, a wine cork, and half a beer-mat. She had found them all in record time, and pleased me. She went indoors, but Josse, who had been in the car while I worked her came out for his exercise and some fun.

I had the cartridge case in my hand, which had been the last thing Chita found, and began to toss it. His eyes focused on it, and he watched. 'That's interesting. What is it?' I hid it in my hand. It smelt of Chita. I put it in my pocket, and he nosed my pocket, becoming more excited.

'What is it? Let me look.'

I didn't. I took it out, threw it up, let him run to me and have a quick sniff, and hid it again. He was becoming more interested. I did this for about ten minutes, never letting him have more than a brief tantalising glimpse of it, or a very quick sniff.

I hid it in my hand, or under my jacket, saying, 'what is it? What have I got? Do you want it then?'

I walked up the field and he followed, trying to put his nose in my pocket.

I turned and began to toss it again, and he began to jump for it, but I didn't let him get near it. His ears were pricked, his eyes very bright and his whole body was alert and interested.

I reached the lawn and threw it. Josse raced to it, and picked it up and galloped back to me. 'Look at me. Aren't I clever?' I said so, with all the enthusiasm I could muster, and took it from him. I threw it again and this time he swanked.

From that day on I always had a cartridge case in my pocket and played with it with him for a little while, never long enough for him to lose interest. I could not throw it far; that didn't trigger him at all. It had to be within three feet of me. Imperceptibly the distance lengthened, until, just over a year after I had had him, when I took him with me on my annual visit to the Show at Findon Downs, I had the cartridge case in my pocket.

At the end of the Show, when we were clearing up and all the other dogs had gone home, Josse and Chita came out with the whole rugby field to themselves. Chita found a branchlike pole and proceeded to make up for being penned most of the day and race around with it in her mouth. She had problems as it was very big, and she couldn't find the point of balance.

Josse clung to me. This was a big place, and there was the clubhouse, and I just might be going to take him into that, hand him over to someone he didn't know, and vanish.

I tossed the cartridge case about ten feet from me. Josse raced to it, picked it up and brought it back. On a strange field among strange people, as about twenty of us were removing rings, clearing litter, making sure no valuables were left.

I was helping load all the gear into our three cars, as I stay with the Show secretary and the Show treasurer, with Josse, as always, desperately anxious if out of the car in new surroundings, shadowing me at every step. Chita kept an eye on me but was happy to run around at a distance, though as soon as I went to my car she was there, just in case I got in and forgot her. As I walked back for the next load, I flicked the cartridge case, over and over, and Josse raced to it and brought it back.

I stopped before he grew tired of the game. It was an enormous step forward, as he had several times had people he didn't know within a few feet of him as he ran out. In the early months he'd have run to the car. The door was open so that he could get in.

He didn't bother. He was enjoying himself.

Only the two friends I stay with knew what a big step this was for this dog, and that today real progress had been made.

Another friend, to whom I wrote a few weeks later, saying he was also now retrieving strips of leather the saddler saves for me, made him a small leather gundog dummy, of very soft material, with a soft stuffing. This was pocket-sized. I kept it with me and I threw it when I sat down, I threw it when we went out, and Josse adored it.

We did not yet have the formal competition retrieve where the dog sits and waits for a command, then runs out, fetches, brings the object back and sits again holding it. I had no intention of teaching that for a long time yet, as it is the quickest way there is of making a dog reluctant to retrieve. Why race out when you have been told to stay for several seconds, when the urge was there? By then, it's gone, until the dog is a long way into his training and has become hooked on fetching, no matter how long you prevent him from running out. I didn't want to sour him, and to make him wait to retrieve just as he was beginning to enjoy doing so, would do just that.

If he showed signs of refusing, I stopped the game, and then, later, threw the dummy and fetched it myself, not allowing him to get it. By the time I had reached it, before he had, about five times he was thoroughly frustrated and the sixth time I let him win it.

If we were to compete one day he had to retrieve a dumb-bell. I tried him with a wooden one. He loathed it. I tried a plastic one, and he loathed that. I could by now get him to pick up anything else, even pens and books and rulers, but not the dumb-bell.

I tried putting it in his mouth. He panicked again, and showed signs of stress. I wondered if his fifth owner, who had intended to do protection work with him, had taught him or tried to teach him to take a dumb-bell and maybe hurt his mouth. Protection work at its higher stages can mean learning to bite on a padded sleeve, for criminal work, but I doubted if Josse had progressed as far as that before he was sold to Eric. If he had, his mouth might have been hurt when he tugged. His teeth weren't good when I got him and he is still reluctant to eat really hard dog biscuits.

I rang the saddler. He is a very obliging man, who, in spite of losing a leg in the Falklands war, teaches his own spaniels gundog work and goes shooting. So he understands the difficulties of dog training.

Whenever I go over for the club leads he makes, which are

far superior to any sold in pet shops, he produces all kinds of leather offcuts for Chita's searches.

Had he any soft leather? Could he stitch it round the dumb-bell stem?

No problem.

I took Josse's leather dummy with me, to show him what it was made of and he found a piece to match, and bound it round the plastic stem, and stitched it, making such a neat job that it is invisible. There are no rules as to what a dumb-bell should be made of for shows.

I threw the dummy, and Josse fetched it, always indoors. Out of doors was something else and there was always something more interesting. A bird would fly over and he'd watch it. Or the search and rescue helicopter would pass overhead, on its way to the mountains and distract him until that was out of sight. Indoors, there was nothing to distract him.

He fetched the dummy four times. I put it away and took his dumb-bell, holding the two ends in my hands, hidden, so that he could only see the stem. He sniffed it. That's interesting. He sniffed it again. He took it in his mouth, and sat with it. I put it on the floor and he nosed it, and picked it up.

I hid it behind me. He tried to find it. I hid it under my jersey and he began to be excited. I sat on it, and he thought that hilarious and sat, tongue lolling, eyes laughing at me. Chita found all this a bore. She came to see what we were doing and went back to her bed.

I threw the dumb-bell a couple of feet, and Josse pounced on it, and then dropped it. We started again, and this time he held it long enough for me to take and praise him. Last thing at night, for weeks, we played with that dumb-bell, Josse gradually holding it longer, gradually bringing it further, gradually carrying it round the room while I heeled him.

It took almost a year to get the exercise right indoors. Out of doors, he would fetch the cartridge case and fetch the dummy. He would run to the dumb-bell, and sniff it, and then run off. On-lead, he'd simply sit down.

'We play that game in the sitting-room, not the garden.'

Then, one evening, when I took Josse into club, I tried him

with the dumb-bell and he fetched it from a couple of feet away from me, bringing it in perfectly. I tried in the garden next day.

Not he.

Even now, he will not always go for it, and never if it is more than three feet away from me, and then only on the lawn. Not in long grass, which is the more usual type of ground for Trials. There's still a very long way to go there.

Until he fetches reliably the search is also only a hope. He will fetch any small object I throw into the search ring, but if it is lying still, he will nose it, and trot off. 'What am I supposed to do with that?'

So he is learning to search indoors. I have reached the stage where I can show him the cartridge case, let him play with it, until he is very excited, then hide it in my pocket and tease him with a glimpse of it. 'Where's it gone? Do you want it? Not yet.' He gets more and more eager, more and more curious, pushing against me, sniffing the pocket and my hand, and when he is so excited that I know it will work, I put him on a sitstay, go into another room and hide the cartridge case, and then send him for it.

At first he found that a bewildering game but now he waits for it, dashes in and searches busily and brings me his trophy. 'Clever boy.' It is one of Chita's favourite games so they take it in turns.

One day it will all come together.

Meanwhile he is making me more and more inventive and that is helping dogs in club as we have several non-retrievers there, one of them a gundog!

Chapter Fifteen

Like many other people, I enjoy going on courses. There are all kinds in the dog world, most given by those successful in competition, either in Obedience or Working Trials, who want to pass on their knowledge.

I found these interesting and often learned new training tips. I often found too that those giving them knew a great deal about training and very little about dogs, which was a bit surprising. The majority of them owned Collies, as these have become the Rolls-Royces of the dog working world, owing to the ease with which those carefully bred dogs train.

With this takeover has come changes in the style of work done and higher expectations of the standard expected, as the Collie is fast, accurate and willing. When I take a Collie on the floor at club, after struggling with some of the other breeds, it feels like a feather, light, biddable and very easy to manage.

I found most of the courses were limiting because of this. I didn't want to know how to work a Collie. I wanted to know a great deal about all kinds of dogs, and all kinds of work involving dogs. I couldn't find the type of course I wanted.

I found, too, that there were often people on those courses with a vast interest in dogs who had come hoping to find companionship and maybe also understanding help with a specific problem. They rarely did. Many of the courses had far too many people on them. It is tempting to fill up, and take the money, as it is in club. Some were badly organised. Others were a waste of time.

Of the twelve I have been on, four were extremely valuable. The others I could have run better myself, and I would have limited the numbers. Crowded classes teach nothing, and crowded courses are self-defeating, so it is far more valuable to limit both. A number of the courses were very boring, with nothing new to offer, and a great deal of time wasted. Once I made the mistake of going back a second time and discovered that though during the years I had read a great deal of new research on training, those taking the course were rooted in the past and had nothing new to offer at all. I had no intention if I did repeat my course of doing the same thing year by year, as there is always so much new information flooding in from research organisations all over the world concerned with dogs, their breeding, their well-being, and their training.

Sometimes those who were relatively new to dog-owning but very anxious to learn more were right out of their depth. What was being taught was fine if you wanted to win Cruft's, but like me, that wasn't one of their ambitions.

Like me, they didn't have the type of dog that could win Cruft's, and like me, their dog was their dog, for a lifetime. Not to be passed on because it couldn't work, or wouldn't win the higher classes, or wasn't clever enough. And like me, they hadn't room for more than three dogs at most, if that.

One day I was having a beef about this to a dog-minded friend who has also had a rescued dog. I hadn't got Josse then. It was about two months before he loomed on my horizon.

'Why don't you run your own course?' she asked.

I stared at her. I had never thought about that. If I did run the course, I stood to gain as much as anyone, because I knew just what I wanted to do on it. I titled it 'A Course with a Difference', aimed it at novice dog owners, not the top people, who in any case were unlikely to come on any course I ran, as I have never won any top prizes in either Trials or Obedience, and began to make plans.

The plans took time, as there was a great deal to organise. I needed a venue, and one I could afford. Though I had no intention of making a fortune out of this, I would need to charge, as I intended asking various people in the dog world to come and talk to us, and they would need expenses, if not a fee.

I put an advertisement in *Dog Training Weekly*. If nobody answered, then I would give up the idea.

I had more replies than I expected and so had to begin to make the course a reality.

I did not then know it would be complicated by Josse, who I would have owned for some four months at the time, and who would still be in a very stressed state.

Chapter Sixteen

If I were to hold a course I had a great deal of planning to do.

The venue was the first thing to consider. Recently the local pub in our village had changed hands, the new owners Phyllis and Chris Morley coming from Stockport, not far from where we used to live, so we soon found we had much in common from old memories. Also they own four rescued Setters, three Irish and one English, and Phyllis had come to club briefly with Cindy, and brought her on to the TV programme, though once she got busy in the season she had to give up dog club, as the Setters do meals.

I went to see them, and we arranged that they should provide facilities. We could have the snug for our lectures, one of the fields for our training, and Phyllis and Kay, her daughter, would provide a midday meal at a special price for us, and also evening meals for myself and our lecturers. We could have the venue free.

There was no problem about dogs as they love animals. Over the years since they have been here the pub has acquired a goat; four little calves too young to be sold, that were probably originally destined for veal; a quantity of drakes, which was a mistake, as half of them at least should have been ducks; and chickens. We spend a lot of time leaning over fences watching the animals when I go to arrange something there. They have been very supportive of all our activities including that of collecting for the club Guide Dogs for the Blind.

There was a lot of organising to do. My first thought was to have a variety of people: a shepherd with his sheep and sheepdogs; mountain rescue dogs; protection dogs, which Eric would bring; the little bomb sniffer that Les Edwards had recently acquired for the North Wales police; a blind man and his dog.

The day was to be divided into three sections. In the mornings there would be talks; in the afternoons demonstrations or practical work, and lectures with videos, by visitors in the evening.

A friend who has a television shop offered to lend me a video player and monitor for nothing. Needless to say, nothing went quite as planned, there were snags and some things worked out differently, but one of the snags was to bring me three new friends, who were to become a rewarding part of my life.

The course was held in August. I am on the verge of a second one, now, having learned a lot from that first attempt. That will be held later this year.

The first was in the middle of the holiday period. August traffic proved difficult for people coming from a distance, and so was booking in the height of the season. Now the course is being held at the end of September when most places are empty and people are only too pleased to have unexpected late visitors.

The time came at last. One of my most important speakers was David Morgan, who was blinded in an accident many years ago and has had six Guide Dogs. He had just lost Imba, a lovely old German Shepherd and expected to have his new dog by the time the course took place.

With the perversity of fate, the first dog chosen for him wasn't suitable, and the second was not yet ready. She was lent to him, briefly, before her training was completed, for Anglesey Agricultural Show. I met her, an enchanting sixteen-month-old German Shepherd bitch named Gretal (*not* Gretel which is more usual), with the kind of temperament one yearns for. David and his wife Estie fell promptly in love with her and so did their friend Anne, whose cottage is at the bottom of their garden and who is a frequent visitor.

David I already knew slightly as he had accepted a cheque for a thousand pounds, the result of two years fund raising, on the club's behalf for the guide dogs, and we were well into our third collection of £1000. Our first cheque had been accepted by Arthur Rowlands, a North Wales policeman who had been blinded many years ago by a man with a shotgun. His guide dog was also a German Shepherd.

I thought that David's lack of a guide dog would be detrimental but in fact it was quite the reverse. For one thing he had never been without a dog for so long, and was very frustrated. He couldn't get up and go out when he chose, but had to wait till Estie, or Anne, or one of their friends, was free to take him. He spent hours alone where he had been used to having a dog beside him, to stroke and fondle and talk to, while his wife was busy with her housework.

They don't have household help as often those who do help forget that furniture must never be shifted, so that David can find his way without any problems round the house. Move a chair to an unfamiliar place, and he may fall over it and hurt himself badly.

Not that he sat and moaned. Once when I rang up he couldn't answer as he was on the roof of the shed, repairing it. Another time he was making one of the lovely little occasional tables with polished slate tops that he donates for first prizes at any function to raise money for a dog, as he is Anglesey's voluntary organiser. Nobody would ever guess that their maker was blind. He trained as an architect, but is a very good cabinet maker.

So when he spoke about the need of a dog it was very much from the heart, as he had now experienced more than six months without one, and Gretal was not to come to him until five weeks after the course ended.

The members of the course were waiting in the snug when David and Estie and Anne arrived. Anne organises the sale of teacloths, calendars, pens and pencils and all the bits and pieces that can be bought to aid the fund raising and was to hold a car boot sale after David's talk.

David could only walk safely if one of us went in front of him, acting as a dog, and he put his hands on his escort's shoulders, walking behind them, so I was elected guide. He knew the car well, so getting out was simple, but he had to be guided across the car-park and into the pub.

I found it necessary to give a running commentary, or he was in trouble, tripping over the edge of rugs I could see, and he couldn't, or knocking himself against small tables that stuck out further than I realised. Also people had to be warned so that they moved out of our way. The snug lay beyond the bar area, which was packed.

'There's a mat at the door. Lift your feet up. Now turning right, and along a narrow corridor; nothing to bump you. It's a tricky door, opens towards us, hang on.'

We negotiated the door.

'Room full of people, so we'll go slow. Have to dodge them,' as we manoeuvred in a packed room past small tables, elbows, and people with drinks. David wears dark glasses, which are no sign of blindness these days, and he doesn't carry a white stick, as he doesn't normally need it with a dog. I was becoming more adept at talking him past obstacles.

'Turning right, through a narrow gap, into a little room full of people. Have to pass them. Bench here, for you to sit on. The TV set is on your right and Anne has the videos. She's ready to put them on when you tell her.'

It must be very strange, and frequently very unnerving, to be in the dark all the time. Those who once had sight can probably imagine their surroundings but those who have never known it must live in a world that is totally mysterious. Kenneth's uncle went blind a few years before he died, and Monty would hold our hands tightly when we spoke to him, because his greatest fear was that people would walk away, leaving him alone, talking to nobody, and he wouldn't even know he had lost his audience.

David never complains. He gave us a fascinating talk, ending with a poem he had composed on being blind and how indebted the blind are to their dogs. We watched the video which showed how the dogs are puppy-walked, and then how each blind owner meets the dog, and learns how to walk with it. We saw the dog's early training.

We were to have a collection for our own guide dog fund afterwards. I led David out through an even more packed bar, and people stepped aside to watch our progress. When I came back the collection had been started and many of those in the bar asked if they could take part.

Our little journey through the crowd had had a major effect, that would, I think, have had far less impact if David had come with Gretal. Fivers flowed into the collection and we ended up with ten times as much as I had expected and within seven months were able to invite David to accept a cheque for guide dog number three. Our first guide dog, which the club is allowed to name, is called Freya, after a club dog that died young; the second is Puma, after my bitch; and the third is Janus, after my Golden Retriever. Puma is a German Shepherd, but there was not a Golden Retriever ready when Janus was named, and he is a Labrador.

The club has £700 towards the fourth dog, collected in less than six months, as seeing David has proved a great stimulus to everyone, and they are all determined as many people as possible will benefit from the fund raising. We are busy hopefully arguing about a name for guide dog number four.

Gretal since then has become part of David's life. She is not yet two, yet she is fully trained, which is remarkable when you think of the standard of behaviour of most dogs of her breed and her age, often still quite wild and in need of firm discipline. To see them stride out together, you would never know the man was blind except for that white harness on the dog.

We visit often now, but Josse and Chita stay outside in the car, parked in full shade. Josse sometimes sings, because he can't see me, and Gretal runs to the window, puts her paws on the sill and stares out. 'What's wrong with that dog? Where is he?'

David sometimes swanks a little and takes her out on her lead instead of her harness. She did pull at first, but I showed them how to overcome that and she is now a sedate and sensible animal, behaving as well on the lead as on the harness.

Off-lead, she is just a happy, very playful young dog, and when Estie takes her for her romp, she flies against the wind, quite unlike her working self. She walks soberly off-lead by Estie's side till they reach the field where she can run as much as she chooses. She has a great deal of surplus energy to work off. She is an unusually placid and happy dog, but is overcome by the sheer joy of living, and when I visit greets me with restrained excitement, a little moaning murmur and a tiny dance on the spot. She is very like Josse in nature and every time I see her I realise what a marvellous dog he would have been without his change of homes.

Guide dogs are no more perfect than other dogs, being just dogs. Like Josse, Gretal can't bear to be left alone in the car with her owners out of sight, and recently when they went to church for a wedding, they parked the car well away from the building, in case her noise disturbed the ceremony. When they went back to the car David, feeling his way inside said, 'there's something wet here.'

The wetness was the remains of his seat belt; and Estie's had also vanished. Gretal had been stressed by their long absence and like many stressed dogs, had taken out her feelings on the car's upholstery. Peugots are expensive vehicles when it comes to replacements and Gretal's moments of misery cost them a small fortune. It might have been better to take her into church, as guide dogs in particular are so much with their owners of necessity that they may feel unhappy being alone even more than the normal dog.

I knew as soon as that first evening was ended that the course had been well worth while, as there were tips to be picked up on the guide dog video on training, that would not only benefit all who saw it, but also help me with club dogs.

There were poignant moments in the films, such as one woman meeting her dog for the first time. She flung her arms round it and could not bear to let it go. A creature of her own! She lived alone, and the dog was going to make a vast difference to the quality of her life. Another woman, out in the early days of training to walk with her dog, her instructor now at a distance behind her, watching, and ready to step in if needed, brushed against a greengrocers' outside display and knocked a cauliflower to the ground. She stopped, in an empty street, the dog staring at her, and apologised profusely, thinking she had just banged into somebody.

That night, when I took the dogs into the garden, I stood for ages looking up at the sky; at a brilliant moon, casting dappled shadows under the black trees, at a million stars, glittering all over the deep darkness of space; at the white-winged owl flying softly by, and prayed that whatever else lay before me in old age, it wouldn't be blindness.

The dogs came flying in. Josse relaxed as he was at home, though during the day he had barked at other dogs, and cried when I left him. I watched them. Chita, tiny, beautifully made, bright eyed, ears pricked, coming to stare at me, as I was slow with their night-time bread. Josse, still too thin though he was beginning to fill out, nudging my hand, bold now with me, becoming more sure of his place, though he was anxious about the visitors staying in the house. Might they be going to take him away with them? And there was another dog sleeping outside in the car that stood in the drive. Was that going to usurp his place?

John Coley had been among the first people to enrol on the course. I knew him from long ago and had met him on several courses. Also it had been his son's dog which had lain next to Chita when, some years ago, a fight started beside her in the downstay out of sight. Kevin had been bitten and Chita had been terrified and had never stayed when I disappeared ever since. He and his wife, Carol, had had difficulty finding anywhere to stay in the height of the holiday season so they had our spare room. John runs a dog club in Birmingham and is a more dedicated course-goer than anyone I know. He is always anxious to pick up more knowledge, though his own knowledge is deep.

Their presence proved a boon as Carol, who wasn't on the course, took over my home jobs and washed up and shopped, and left me far freer than I would have been otherwise. They are coming again, this time with John helping with the practical instructing.

Our second visitor was Huw the Sheep. Nobody has ever decided whether Huw is a policeman who is a part-time shepherd or a shepherd who is a part-time policeman. He is one of our best North Wales sheepdog trainers, and though he does not compete, the dogs he raises and trains and sells are in high demand.

It had been a very wet summer and we had problems with the field, which was boggy and getting worse as our cars drove in. Huw had a trailer with sheep in it, and had a certain amount of trouble getting that down to the demonstration area. There were more than twenty dogs there, mine and John's in cars, the rest on-lead. All were at a sufficient standard of pet training to lie still when told, and the course members arranged themselves on bales of straw which had been left to act as seats.

The sheep were bouncy, and extremely awkward, a really tough bunch of four. The sheepdog, Roy, was not the dog Huw had intended to bring. He had wanted to bring his bitch, but she was in season. The first thing he said was that he would have to handle Roy in a way that he didn't much like doing in front of novice handlers, as Roy was an exceptionally tough dog who needed an exceptionally tough handler.

Roy was beautifully trained, but he was a handful and he didn't always obey immediately. There was an attraction in the watching crowd, among the dogs, and if Huw relaxed his whistling and shouts (and Roy needed those shouts) the dog would be away from the sheep and nosing his way over to the spectators. We discovered why next day when one of the course Labradors came into heat early. It wasn't much of a problem as all the dogs were leashed and she was watched carefully.

One thing that puzzled me was that when Huw called 'stand' the dog went down, to watch his sheep. I wondered if this was disobedience, as it didn't bother his handler. I asked Huw about it afterwards.

Some sheepdogs do lie down naturally to watch the sheep, but others stand or crouch. Since a shepherd may be handling two dogs together, one of which is a natural croucher, while the other lies down as a matter of course, with the movement inbred, they use one command. To Roy stand actually meant down. To another dog stand meant stand. It simply didn't matter at all. There is little point in forcing a natural croucher to stand erect, or vice versa. Both do the job equally well if trained.

The demonstration was effective as we had a considerable discussion afterwards, which John and I continued when we got home, on the ways of handling dogs, on the amount of voice needed for different dogs, and on the differences needed when handling sensitive dogs, or shy dogs, or nervous dogs, (which aren't necessarily all the same), and the very tough dog which most people never meet.

Roy was very like Chita. Nothing like Josse.

In this area Mountain Rescue is an obvious part of all our lives. I can see the mountains as I turn the corner of the lane which leads to the main road. Looming black and dark against the sky. Tempting the unwary, and sometimes defeating those who are well prepared as they did this year when two climbers, both experienced, both well equipped, died in an avalanche. One of them was the twenty-year-old son of one of my near neighbours in Cheshire. I had known him as a little boy. They were defeated by bad luck, and it seemed such a waste of young lives, but the perils of the great hills will always tempt the brave and adventurous.

I can rarely look at the mountains without thinking of the lives they claim. The search and rescue helicopter flies over, by day and by night, and we know someone else is missing. The mountain rescue Land Rovers pass us as we drive to town. We know they want more dogs, for searching. Like the guide dogs, its a charity, funded by collections.

Roger, one of the mountain rescue team, all of whom must be first class climbers and also hold first class first aid certificates, came with Jet, a dog that had been the hero of many rescues. It could have been any other of the men and women and their dogs, but Jet was off duty that night. All of them have rescues to their credit, and without the dogs many climbers now alive might well have died.

Jet hunted a hidden 'victim' in the demonstration field, using the wind to aid him rather than a track on the ground, going on air scent. Police dogs do this too when they do area searches, or building searches, having to use their noses above ground as well for tracking along the ground.

Puma was a wonderful air scenter, who could get the smell of a squirrel in a tree a hundred yards away and home in on it. She was squirrel crazy. Josse might be but there are fewer squirrels in Wales than in Cheshire and none on our land. We had squirrels galore in our Cheshire garden.

Jet showed us how he wore the harness that anchors him in the helicopter, and we heard how he was trained to stand still when the giant rotors whirr overhead, to jump in and be shackled by the door, to be let down on a winch to search an area without exhausting himself by having to climb to a height beforehand. The waistcoat is specially made with enormously strong shackles, and the dog, lifted by Roger, and swung in the air – as we could hardly have a helicopter on the spot – grinned at us, plainly used to this mode of transport. He was a black Labrador, a chunky happy dog with a wildly waving tail.

The talk, indoors later, was illustrated by magnificent photographs of mountain scenery and told the story of one of the more famous rescues of recent years, one that had a happy ending, when two youngsters went for a mountain walk and were lost.

The training of the dogs makes certain they are sheep-proof, as sheep may jump from a hollow when the dog is searching an area. Sheep live free on the mountains, and there are no walls or fences. Climbers suffering from exposure choose odd places in which to creep and hide. The dog is taught to hunt for his owner first, and then for a stranger to him, cuddled against his owner, hiding in unlikely places, such as under tree trunks, in tiny crevices, under overhangs, or under the scrubby shrubs that cling to the hillside. Finally, volunteer victims, unknown to the dog, hide to give him experience. It is arduous training.

Death is familiar to the mountain men. They meet it too often. Terrible injuries are familiar too, and the dogs must be taught never to touch blood, so that they are trained with rags soaked in pigs' blood, which is nearer to human blood than that of any other animal, and know that they may never lick. They must bark.

At night the dogs wear a harness which has strapped to it a cold light that gives out an eerie glow. This the rescuers watch, as the dog seeks and searches, quartering the territory, which may be vast. It must be strange to lie, perhaps injured, alone, and frightened, and see that glow approach. But to most climbers the sudden warning bark brings immense relief and the knowledge that help is on the way. A stretcher party may be needed, or a helicopter to fly the victim to hospital, but at least the search is over and the climber found.

Few rescues take place in good weather. When the wind screams in our trees, bending them to the ground, and shakes our inner doors though all the windows are latched, and Chia

121

shouts in the night because she is afraid of the noise, there may be, above the wind noises, the throb of an engine and I know there is someone in trouble on the hills, and the men and dogs will be waking as the messages are relayed. Police and mountain rescue are linked and go into instant action and the dogs wake and shake themselves and run to the waiting vans.

At Valley the siren sounds and there is a scramble and the men race to the machines which are serviced day and night and always ready.

There is a brief news item in the papers and on the radio in the morning. Two men died last night on Snowdon. A climber was rescued and is recovering in hospital. They never mention the men who worked through the night in wind, and mist and often snow or the wicked ice they call ver glas, that coats clothes and beards, the dogs' coats and all surfaces and makes the rescue as hazardous for the rescuers as for the victim.

We sleep on, but in the morning meet Bob or Roger or Neil and are told casually, 'We were out last night. It was wicked. But at least the men are safe.'

Or a brief, 'A climber died last night. We couldn't reach him in time.'

Time, in a case of exposure, is critical, and seconds can mean the difference between life and death. So often those who die weren't prepared for the mountains, wearing the wrong clothes, going out on a bright day not knowing that within an instant they can be lashed with all the fury of winter snow. There is often snow on the tops, when down below it is warm and sunny.

By the end of the evening everyone knew a great deal more about a rarely spoken of method of rescue, and a course of dog training that very few ever encounter. That night the listeners dug deep into their pockets and the collection was exceptionally good. That night too those in the bar who had been eavesdropping gave me money afterwards so that I was able to send a second sizeable cheque, to buy equipment that will help those who stake their lives, and maybe can be saved, in the future.

They went off with Jet, and I thought how odd it is that the dog can work so well for men and never ever know just why he does so, or why those people are up on the icy hills, or why he is needed. No matter what work a dog does, he can never know why he does it, or the purpose for which he is used, in man's terms.

The next day was a contrast in some ways, as Les, who was Eric's best man, and whom I had last met at the wedding reception, brought Robbie, a little Springer Spaniel, who is trained to detect explosives. Robbie is a clown. A non-stop working dog, all wagging tail and happy body, so eager that he is hard to restrain. He needs that eagerness, as looking for explosives needs concentration, and he has to work every cranny of a room where some lunatic might have hidden a bomb. He belonged to an elderly lady, who couldn't cope with his energy and offered him to the police.

Robbie had belonged to somebody who couldn't cope with him as he was all energy, a non-stop working dog bred to be out all day with the guns. He had learned one thing thoroughly before Les got him and that was never to jump on furniture. But a bomb-detecting dog has to search furniture, has to jump on windowsills, has to sniff into flowerpots, along mantelpieces, under rugs and carpets, behind cushions, even in the piano. In a hotel he must search every cranny of bathrooms and bedrooms, linen cupboards and store-rooms, wherever a man might hide death.

Les had a mock bomb which he hid in the room inside a basket of logs. Robbie flew round the room, his tail wagging incessantly, as he hunted that special smell that would, he knew, when recognised, bring him what he really wanted, the wonderful game that was his reward.

Over the settles he went, under the chairs, behind the piano, his little nose wrinkling. He was lightening fast as he ran along the windowsills, sniffed in the flowerpots, and under the rugs. He hunted round the giant grate, then empty but full of blazing logs in winter which make the bar especially cosy, and then triumphantly came to a stop, beside the log basket.

His reward was a fervent 'who's a good boy then?' and a game with a small orange quoit that is never out of his handler's pocket, that means far more to Robbie than even a bowl of food.

After that Les gave lessons to those whose dogs had problems, and ended up by being mobbed. Nobody wanted him to go! He is one of the best instructors I have ever met, and his lessons are great fun and very valuable. He, like Eric, enjoys all dogs, and particularly likes the lively bouncy fellows that drive the rest of the dog-training world mad. These are the dogs of character that often turn, if you have the patience to take them on, into the all-time greats.

Les had intended to leave at four but it was seven before he got away.

Eric and Liz arrived next day with Fonz, to show everyone how a protection dog works. Fonz chased Liz, who wore the padded sleeve on which the dog is taught to 'attack', and then Eric 'arrested' her. It was an energetic session for everyone. It is based on police work and the police phrases are used. 'Stop. I want a word with you,' which in fact acts as a trigger to the dog, who as soon as he hears those words knows he has to be in action almost at once.

Eric too gave instruction after his demonstration, and stayed far later than he intended as one member of the course after the other wanted the benefit of his advice. He has been training dogs since he was eleven and is now in his late forties, with years of experience behind him. He began with a relative who was one of the best trainers in the North West, and who proved a hard taskmaster.

The week ended all too soon. On the last night there was a party and a buffet. This caused problems for Phyllis, as Kay, who had been expecting a baby late September, had to go into hospital with complications of pregnancy and gave birth very early, in the middle of the course, to a little girl they named Jasmine. Kay was responsible for working out all the quantities of food needed, and Phyllis apparently spent her time by her daughter's bedside alternately admiring her new granddaughter and asking how much food she needed for forty people.

She managed a magnificent spread, though she did have enough for fifty or more, and there were only thirty of us, but that was easily remedied with big deepfreezes. Anne Malcolm Bentzon, who had come up with Sailor for a long weekend at the start of the course, makes wonderful wedding and christening cakes and had made a beautiful course cake, covered in pale apricot icing, with a centrepiece of lovely tiny flowers, in an enchanting mixed bouquet tied with ribbons, all of icing sugar. It took pride of place on the table, which looked extremely festive. Chris, Phyllis's husband, suggested we toasted the new baby, and it turned into a very merry evening. One of the members had composed a course song, which everyone sang to me, to the tune of 'After the Ball is Over', much to the astonishment of those in the bar.

It had been a bonus week for Josse, as not only had he had John and Carol there in the house all the time, the first time he had known visitors who stayed, and didn't vanish at bedtime, but Anne had been there with Sailor for three days as well, and he had to contend with another dog in the house. That hadn't been entirely successful and there were two three-cornered fights, every time when we allowed the dogs to meet in a confined space like a passage or porch. We soon learned better.

Anne hadn't met Josse before as I had left him with Eric when Chita and I went South for Findon Downs show.

Josse had had an entirely new experience all week. He had come out of the car to work with other dogs when both Les and Eric were there, and had accepted them. He had been doing very well indeed, and I had felt then that he would soon settle down to be a normal dog, but I had not reckoned with a bad fight later, or what was to prove a major disaster, though at first it seemed only a minor nuisance.

Chapter Seventeen

Life never seems to run smoothly for very long. I was feeling fit; Josse was making progress; I was looking forward for the first time for years to a Christmas free from work. No proofs to correct, and time to prepare and enjoy the shopping, cooking, and buying and parcelling of presents.

It was early November, and one of those rare bright days when the sun shines over the Straits and the water is smooth and calm. There was snow on the tops, outlining the mountains which always brood on the horizon.

I had planned the afternoon. A visit to the bank, then to the vet to pick up some pills for the cat, who had one of her intermittent tummy problems. At nearly fifteen she was doing very well, but old age does bring troubles in its wake, and few animals avoid them. The same symptoms had bothered her twice before, so there was no urgency. I knew what was needed and when it was needed and Chia could stay happily at home, as she hated travelling in the car.

Three weeks before I had been bogged down when I went to train the dogs. The field had looked solid; it had felt solid when I walked in it, but cars are much heavier than people, and there, when I drove in, I stuck. Our local policeman saw me, fetched the farmer and his tractor and we were dragged out of the mud and on to firm ground again. Now, as I drove, I heard a very odd noise coming from the rear of the car.

Had the dragging damaged the vehicle? Was I losing a wheel? Or the exhaust system? Or was I about to break down? I came to a layby, and decided I had better turn in as the road was not very wide and if I did break down I would be a hazard. I began to slow, preparatory to signalling, stopping, and turning. I knew there was traffic behind me, so used the far end of the layby, rather than the near end, as that would have meant very sudden slowing down.

A moment later, the car seemed to explode. The hatchback shot up, I lost the pedals, and we were coasting downhill, fortunately at a slow pace, as I had been almost stationary when the noise occurred. It sounded like the knell of doom. Chita, on the seat beside me, was curled up, pretending she wasn't really there at all. Josse stood behind me, shaking his head slightly. I could see him in the mirror, which had mysteriously become misaligned, but the only other thing that I could see was the back of the hatchback, at the most extraordinary angle.

I couldn't find the brakes. I didn't know what had happened, and I had banged my head. The car was still moving. I wasn't driving. I didn't even have my hands on the wheel, and not only was there no brake, but the clutch and accelerator pedals had vanished too. My foot felt round in empty air. I didn't feel frightened. I didn't feel anything. I remembered the handbrake and put it on. I eased the car to the kerb and stopped. I didn't think I dared stand. I didn't appear to have any legs. I put my hand on Chita, who was shaking.

A woman put her head in at the window, which I had opened, why I didn't know. It just felt more spacious and less shut in.

'Are you all right?' she asked.

'I don't know.' I felt very odd indeed.

'Do you need an ambulance?' That was the last thing I needed. What would happen to the dogs?

'What happened?' I asked.

'The car behind ran into you.'

She vanished, to disappear for ever, leaving behind her an impression of a dream. I was dazed, and not at all sure I would ever be able to move again. I was puzzled, and couldn't work out what I ought to do next. I sat on, alone, aware the woman had said something about the police. Maybe they would come and help me. Nobody else seemed in the least interested in me.

After what seemed like a year, but was probably only about ten minutes, I got out. I looked at my car in disbelief. It hadn't got a back, just a crumpled mass of metal. The rear window had come out at the bottom, the hatchback was doubled in two, the bumper had been driven into the back of the car. The rear lights were smashed. I had been hit fair and square, and obviously the impact had sent me down the road. Luckily there was nothing else coming.

Behind me was a large heavy car with the front pushed in, and an angry man beside it. He said his chest hurt. I didn't think I was hurt, but I knew I was very shocked. My legs still felt as if they were made of paper.

The dogs had cuddled down. Chita seemed half her normal size, and did not bark even when a policeman put his head through the window and looked at her. Josse was also curled nose to tail, and ominously quiet.

A friend of mine passed, on his way to the garage where I had bought my car. He came to see that I was not hurt, and offered to ask them to send a breakdown van. That would be one problem solved. We made statements to the police. I felt removed from reality, trapped in a bad dream.

The police were both kind and considerate. There were two of them. One suggested I drove my car into the layby. I got in, and tried to reverse. I still couldn't reach the pedals. The car seemed to have elongated. Then I realised the seat was in the wrong position. It must have shot back on impact. I shifted it, and found I was shaking so violently I couldn't do anything. One of the policemen reversed the car.

Neither dog took the slightest notice of him.

The garage sent a breakdown van with room in it for both me and the dogs. I led Chita out. She came, on her lead, like a lamb, got into the strange van, and curled up again behind the passenger seat, on the floor among a load of scattered tools.

When I went to take Josse out I found the crash had dented his cage. The door was jammed, and wouldn't open, and Josse by now was panicking, wanting to be out and with Chita again. One of the policemen tried to open the door. It was truly stuck. We considered it. In the end three men kicked together and the door flew open and the dog leaped out. I was just in time to grab his collar, and lead him over to the pick-up. I was sure he would never settle, especially as my car was his sanctuary, but once free of his cage, and with Chita, he lay down with his nose on her back and remained still.

Neither dog moved while the tow chain was fixed. Nor did

they bother when the driver got in. We were not far from the garage. The first thing they did was to take me inside, feed me strong sweet coffee, and make me sit and rest. The dogs remained in the pick-up while my car was unhitched. They seemed to have no energy and I certainly had none. We had to empty my car, which contained dogs' leads and training equipment and dog club gear, which I stored there to save loading and unloading every week.

Then we were driven home.

Kenneth was out, but came back before my driver had left, and was shocked to hear what had happened. 'If you hadn't had a Volvo you might have been very badly injured or dead,' one of the policemen had said. I couldn't get the words out of my mind.

Kenneth took over the dogs' feeding, as they certainly hadn't lost their appetites, which was one good sign, and he also prepared Chia's tiny meal. I sometimes look at her plate, after feeding the dogs and wonder if we starve her, but she only weighs seven pounds. Chita weighs fifty-six pounds, and Josse is well over ninety pounds. He made a meal for us. I didn't want to do anything and I didn't seem able to think properly. I couldn't even imagine how I would manage without a car. It would be weeks before mine was ready to use again.

'You need a hire car and get back on the road, fast,' Kenneth said. It was a principle I was used to, as every time I fell off a horse I had to get straight back on. If you don't, you may give up. Fear gains the upper hand, and it is far harder to conquer if you don't get straight into the saddle. I didn't much like the thought of a hire car but I needed one in which I could travel to the dogs, or they would be de-socialised, left at home, going nowhere.

A number of phone calls produced a firm that had a Morris Ital for hire. I seemed to be living on the phone, reporting to insurers, sorting out strange details, looking up car licence numbers and engine capacity and long involved policy numbers, and also writing letters which needed complex reference numbers at the beginning. I was very glad I had a computer, as I could put all the details into its memory and bring them back at will, like magic.

Two days after the accident I collected the Ital, and decided to take the dogs to the vet for a check-up as both were still very subdued.

The dogs decided otherwise. They were not going in the car, not any car, not ever again. Cars made horrible noises and dogs got stuck in cages. They had to go in. They ran round the house. They ran into the house. They sat, their tails firmly rooted to the ground, and resisted every movement I made. Finally I dragged them in, and tied each by the lead to the rear of the car, to the supports to which the back seats normally fastened when up. I had converted it to the estate version.

Chita panicked and I put her in front with me, where she usually travelled. Josse, after a few moments, decided he had to be sensible. He is basically an extremely sensible dog. However the accident had affected him in more ways than one as, a couple of days later, when I took Chita out of the car, in the park, to do some training with her, his nerviness returned and he chewed the front passenger seat belt right through. I shortened his lead. The hire car cost enough without adding Josse-damage.

On that first day, once the dogs were settled, I drove up to our gate and into the lane, and out onto the village street.

A car came up behind us, far too close. I prayed at it, willing it to fall back. Josse raved at it. He had occasionally barked in the car but never like this. The noise was deafening and he would not stop. He did not intend to have any car behind us, close, and his idea of close was within a hundred-yard range. Worse, he now also barked at people on the pavement, and at cars passing in the opposite direction. It was a nightmare drive.

It is only ten miles to our vet, but it felt like a hundred. He examined them both carefully. Neither dog was hurt, physically, and it wasn't possible to tell if Chita was harmed mentally. Josse very definitely was.

I bent to hold Chita and found as I did so that my neck hurt like hell. I could barely move for a moment. The doctor had examined me the day before and found nothing but some bruising from the seat belt. My neck hadn't hurt then.

'Whiplash,' said my vet when I got my breath back, and told him about it. 'It often doesn't develop for a day or two; after the accident you are numb with shock. People often feel nothing for a couple of days and then develop pains on the third day. Go back to the doctor.'

There was no surgery till next day. It seemed wise to drive, just drive, choosing quiet roads, and traversing the island, to get my nerve back and to get the dogs used to the car again. I couldn't do with dogs that couldn't travel.

I couldn't work. My neck hurt too much, in spite of the pills the doctor had given me. I couldn't reverse in narrow spaces, as my head couldn't turn to the right at all without an agonising amount of pain. Kenneth had to put my car away for the next few weeks. I could only read if I held the book high.

Somehow I went on teaching. I could do it standing still, not moving my head, walking round people I wanted to talk to, to get in the right position, and I took care not to handle the dogs. Meanwhile my own dogs were suffering badly from lack of training. And also there was the PAT (Pro-dogs Active Therapy) dinner, and Chita and I were due to go to that by train.

It was less than three weeks after the crash. I didn't feel at all well, and I couldn't move my head more than a few inches to either side. It was far too painful. I had also hurt my ankle; another injury I only discovered after a few days. Kenneth thought the change would do me good, and give me something else to think about. I still couldn't work, as it was too painful to keep my head up and watch the computer monitor.

I drove over to Eric's.

Josse was to stay with him. I left the car at Callanway with relief – Josse still told off every driver who came too near, and his idea of near was not the same as mine at all. For all that, I hadn't got my own nerve back, and the motorway terrified me, as every driver seemed to be far too close, and if he wasn't, Josse thought he was. I could get some relief from the dog's barking by telling him to lie down. If he did that he couldn't see the other cars until they were almost on us.

We arrived at lunchtime. Liz, Eric's wife, now several months pregnant to their delight, fed us, and we spent a leisurely afternoon chatting and watching television. Josse had not wanted to go in his kennel. He grabbed my jacket and held on, and when I removed that from his mouth, he took my wrist. We persuaded him to let go, and he went, very reluctantly, back to his familiar one-time home.

Eric drove us to the station for the London train. It was a Saturday night and a football train. Though nobody was obstreperous I was astounded by the amount they drank, each table rapidly filling up with cans and bottles, glasses replenished time after time after time, and voices growing noisier and laughter more raucous. I learned some astonishing things about the private lives of my fellow passengers. Chita, who had never been on a train before, curled under the table.

I presented her ticket.

'Where's the dog?'

'Under the table.'

He bent down. 'My God, it's an Alsatian!' Chita gave him a disgusted look and went back to sleep.

Though it is only just over two hours from Macclesfield to London, unlike the Irish Mail from Holyhead which takes nearly five hours, it seemed a long journey. Nobody minded me queueing for the buffet with a dog. Only one person was afraid of her. By the end of the journey even the guard was petting her.

She did not like Euston station. It was busy and there were more people than she had seen in her life, rushing around in every direction. I was loaded with a handbag and a large case, containing her food and bowl and blanket for her bed, as well as my own clothes and party outfit.

A porter took pity on me and that problem was quickly solved. The taxi driver raised an eyebrow, but I assured him she would behave and would lie on the floor, and not on his seats.

The hotel had been booked by Pro-dogs. Chita was the 1000th PAT dog, and she was to receive a badge of honour at a banquet on the Sunday evening at the Grosvenor banqueting rooms in Willesden.

She was used to hotels, but this had no garden and we had to take a taxi ride to the heath for Chita's benefit. Once this was done we went back to our room, which was up on the fourth floor and hotter than either of us liked, even with the window wide open. I fed Chita and put down her rug, then went to find my own food.

The staff were friendly, especially the porters, and they liked dogs. I was not the only dog owner there, but the other dogs were there for a Breed show, to find the Pro-dog Dog of the Year from among a number of starring champions. No one had heard of PAT dogs, so I explained that it stood for Pro-dogs Active Therapy, and that the dogs are used in hospitals, homes and nursing homes to provide stimulus and affection for those without dogs, especially those who once had them and now have to live without.

Medical research has now proved what those of us who work with dogs already knew: that dogs are a major benefit for those living alone, for children, and for the elderly, providing uncritical companionship, affection and approval in a world that is very trying to live in indeed, and often frightening as well as frustrating.

Animals live in the real world and can never live anywhere else. They may accept the environment we provide, but they see it through their noses, and their sensations. They never understand all we say but they do understand all we do, and if we are clever enough to make deed and word coincide then we have clever dogs.

I walked Chita after my meal, along lamp-lit streets, a little worried lest we meet with someone bent on mischief, but our only encounter was with a startled tabby cat that came out of a gateway and stared, and sped over the wall before Chita had time to register that this was a cat. Usually she is good, and does not chase them, unlike Josse who is still triggered if he sees any cat other than Chia.

It is lonely in a strange town in a strange hotel. I looked at television, at programmes I would never normally bother to watch and went to bed early, to read the last despatch on the therapeutic value of animals, especially with the mentally handicapped, from the Society for the Study of the Companion Animal.

It was difficult for both Chita and me to sleep. It was so hot. It was a relief to wake at seven in the morning and get up and take her out. I started to walk to the heath, and found it a long and uphill trail, and my neck was hurting abominably. I hailed a taxi, and we finished the journey in style and he waited for us to walk, kindly switching off his meter to give the dog a real chance of some exercise.

After breakfast I found, to my delight, that Chita could come into the lounge where there were other dogs and owners. The morning passed fast, talking about gundog work versus working trials, talking dog, endlessly. I had to dress ready for the evening, so I found myself at 2 pm back on Hampstead Heath, walking Chita dressed in black velvet trousers, a lacy nylon blouse and a thick overcoat and feeling remarkably cold. Then we were off to the banqueting rooms, to press and radio interviews, and to meet new people.

Chita was fascinated. She had never seen such a place. All those tables with white cloths and flowers, and delicious food. All those people in long dresses, smelling of scent. I wondered if she liked the kind of perfume that humans apply to themselves. Her small nose was lifted, sniffing endlessly. She curled at my feet while we ate cucumber sandwiches and discussed dogs. What else? It is the prestige gathering of the year, an event that will be remembered for ever by those who go.

Then came disaster. Chita could not stay with me during the banquet. She would receive her medal afterwards, but meanwhile she had to go out and be fastened to a bench in the vestibule, while I left her with two lovely girls from the Battersea Dogs' Home.

Chita had never been benched. The other dogs, veterans of many shows, titled beauties, champions all, looked down their aristocratic noses at this extraordinary animal that cried like a puppy as I left. The girls assured me she would settle and they could manage, and they had several bags of titbits with which to pacify her.

My table was in the middle of the room but for all that I was sure I heard her wails several times during the meal that followed, and the speeches after it. Katie Boyle, who is really Lady Saunders, was on the top table in the most beautiful black velvet dress, with a skirt like an inverted tulip. As always she looked enchanting.

At last the coffee was served, the speeches were ended and we could fetch our dogs. Chita had to come off the bench as she almost pulled it down. She was sitting with one of the girls, being cuddled, but still whining. She had eaten all the titbits. She saw me and launched herself at me. How could you leave me in a strange place with strange people?

There were other dogs to receive awards. The sheepdog that had rescued a number of sheep and horses from a fire, carrying on with his work although he had been badly affected by smoke. He was a big handsome dog, as at home in the ballroom as in the farmyard, and wandered happily off-lead, going up to people to be fussed. After him came a little mongrel that had almost been put to sleep, but was rescued. He had smelt gas and refused to stop barking, and his action saved a whole road from an explosion.

Then it was our turn and Chita trotted beside me, up to the platform, to receive our plaque and her medal to wear, sure she was the centre of attraction as indeed she was, though not in the same way. She posed for her photograph. She knew all about that.

It was late and I was very aware of my feet, as I had discovered, with the ankle injury, I had a choice of wearing the shoes that went with my evening clothes and not being able to walk at all, or keeping on my heavy out-and-about shoes and being able to move. I decided it was not much use becoming chairbound, and opted for the heavy shoes. They didn't go with my outfit and I hoped everyone was too busy with their own affairs to notice them. Such silly things can bother one on great occasions.

The evening ended excitingly with the choice of the Champion of the Year from among eighteen dogs, all champions. They walked regally and I was glad I wasn't judging.

The honours went to the beautiful flatcoated retriever. Suddenly the evening was over and carriages were at the door. Mine was a minicab with a driver who had never heard of my hotel, and as I was in strange country I couldn't direct him. Worse, his base had never heard of the hotel either. I knew it was off the Finchley Road and I knew that the road it was in led up to Hampstead Station. And that was all I knew. It was well after midnight, my neck was aching, and both Chita and I were exhausted.

There was nobody about to ask. We drove up side roads, we drove along the Finchley Road and back; and then suddenly I saw a familiar crossing. Chita and I had waited there to hail a taxi that afternoon. We were home, or at least, at our temporary home. It was exactly 1 am when I said goodnight to the porter.

It was a cool night. Chita had been exercised in the waste ground behind the banqueting rooms so did not need to go out. We both slept, and the alarm clock, waking us for a train at 8 am was an intrusion.

Pro-dogs had made our visit memorable by giving me an enormous beautiful flowering azalea in a basket. I finished breakfast and commandeered the porter. I couldn't manage Chita, the stairs, heavy bag, handbag and an azalea in a basket. I trotted down like a lady with my dog and my potted plant, and was followed by my luggage.

The taxi driver appreciated my well-behaved dog and found me an Irish porter at Euston. There was time to spare as London had been half empty at that time of day. A lad in jeans and a dirty white anorak and equally dirty white sneakers came up and asked if he could talk to my dog. When I said yes, he sat beside her, his arms round her, and buried his face in her fur. He told Chita, not me, that he had a dog like her at home, that he missed his dog, that he couldn't get a job at home, and he was living in a hostel which was no fun at all. He asked her how old she was and listened to my answer and told her she didn't look nearly nine.

Then his train was called and he kissed her goodbye and vanished, without ever once looking at me. I thought that Chita had probably performed her first task as a PAT dog.

A lonely and unhappy boy had spent a few minutes enjoying her closeness, her affection, and her undemanding presence.

The porter took us to the train and found a seat for me, with a table under which Chita could lie, and very carefully arranged my azalea so that it wouldn't fall or be damaged. It looked remarkably festive, with its scarlet flowers and little bows that read Pro-dogs.

It was windy at Macclesfield and there weren't any porters. I arranged myself carefully, with Chita on my left and the azalea in the same hand as her lead. That way I could manage. It was a long platform, but Chita was angelic, and as we walked I devised a club test with everyone having to walk their dogs carrying a large case, a handbag and an azalea in a basket, up the steps on to the stage, across it and down the other side. Liz had come to meet me. Josse had been good. London was a memory and we were back in our familiar surroundings. Josse, brought out of his kennel, careered round me, crying, and nibbling at me, almost eating me with joy.

He went into the car with Chita, and once more Liz fed me, before we began on our journey home. It was a wretched journey with pouring rain and Josse barking, and worse, the engine overheating all the way. When Kenneth looked at it next day he found it almost waterless, with a major leak.

We returned the car, with him driving behind me with a water carrier, wondering why the thing hadn't blown up on the way back from Macclesfield. We had to fill it up three times in fourteen miles.

I was without a car again. The insurers were still arguing; should they repair my car or write it off? And until they decided I did not know what to do. I would buy a new Volvo if mine were written off, so went to Tyn Lon garage, at Llanfair PG, the village with a name too long to use. They had helped me at the time of the accident, and helped me with the insurance letters, and my wrecked car was still in their storage garage.

They could hire me a car, but it wouldn't be usable by the dogs. It was in good condition, and was a small saloon. There was no room for dogs although Chita could ride with me, if I covered the front seat, when she needed the vet. Josse had cost me thirty pounds extra on the Ital for a new seat belt. The vet would have to come to him, and of course, in the next few weeks, Josse was ill, and I had to ask for a house visit. No one else had a car for hire that would take the dogs. It would mean the dogs couldn't go out again except round our home, until I had a new car, or a repaired car.

I had no choice. You can't live here without a car, as the nearest shops are ten miles away. We can't buy clothes or meat or fish or Christmas presents and Christmas was nearly upon us and once more would be a rush and a problem, instead of the fun I had hoped. My neck hurt more than ever, and I was booked to have an X-ray. I had visions of my spine being broken and my head dropping off and once said so to someone at the dog club, jokingly, and was told, absurdly, that Tchaikovsky was always afraid his head would fall off when he conducted so he held it on!

It was a ridiculous thought that comforted me in the weeks to come as it made me laugh. I took the little blue Volvo, for what I thought would be just a few days.

It turned out to be seven weeks. And that was a disaster, as at the end of seven weeks Josse had become completely unused to cars, to people, and to other dogs, and I was back where I started with him, right at the beginning, except that he no longer fence-ran bullocks.

He lunged at other dogs. He behaved like a maniac in club, and he barked at every one who came near me, whether he was in the car, on his lead in the street, or in the park. I dared not let him off-lead. I didn't know what he would do.

That car crash was not only a major nuisance, but far more of a disaster than I had thought. However, I was sure Chita couldn't become desocialised. Not at her age. I was wrong.

Chita, on her first walk through Beaumaris, to the bookshop, was absolutely terrified of passing cars. She had never been traffic-shy. I was to curse that road accident for the next few months, as it gave me far more trouble than I ever anticipated, and the kind of trouble that only a dog owner would understand. I had gone so far with Josse and made so much progress, and now it was all to do again.

Life just wasn't fair.

Chapter Eighteen

I had learned a lot from Josse's behaviour in the Volvo that had been wrecked. After weeks of argument, the insurers decided it was a write-off and I began to organise its replacement. I didn't realise, at first, that the accident had done me more harm than I knew. All I was aware of was the fierce and constant pain in my neck, that had prevented me from using my computer for over seven weeks, as I simply couldn't keep my head in one position for very long.

I wasn't aware that I had been suffering for months from a total inability to concentrate, and also had other injuries. This was because they were not nearly so noticeable as that whiplash in my neck, which simply never eased, day or night, in spite of constant doses of painkiller, which was the only treatment I had till I went for acupuncture, which cured it. I was still exhausted after every drive and it was months before I completely regained my nerve.

The X-rays showed massive bruising, but no breakages, which was a relief. The letters went on – with the insurance company, over the car, as they had offered me less than its worth, and with a solicitor, provided by the RAC, who was involved in trying to get me back the money I had spent on the hired car, and some damages for the injuries. That, almost a year later, still isn't settled, though the accident was in no way my fault. It was a straight run into from the rear. A hire car for seven weeks cost a fortune and I'd been assured I'd get my money back.

Everyone at the Volvo garage seems to have a dog. A pointer, a Rottweiler, so that my insistence on having my new car geared for the dogs was understood perfectly. Chita, who had never been caged in the car, since she was a younster, was to have her own compartment. She had been unprotected, and could have been seriously hurt.

I had the new car adapted before I took it. The rear seat, (it is another Volvo hatchback) was removed, a ply floor put in, the centre divided, and a couple of cages built. The doors had their panels removed, and wood substituted. Josse promptly ate the wood on his side, so it went back for aluminium panels, which prevented that happening.

The rear is heavy weldmesh, so made that on hot days the hatchback can be opened and the dogs are secure, but can get plenty of air. Chita to my surprise, behaved as if she had always travelled that way.

Neither dog had been in the car for weeks. Neither dog wanted to get in the car, but they had to learn again to travel, or my life would be too restricted. I drove them round the island, and found myself positively neurotic about that rear mirror. Whenever a car came close I told it to get back; I still couldn't bear anyone behind me.

Chita lay quiet, not looking out of the window, not moving, apparently anchored to the floor. Josse didn't. He prowled as well as he could in that restricted space, turned and turned again, and he barked.

He barked at cars behind us, at bicycles beside us at road junctions, at people walking on the pavements, and he went demented whenever he saw another dog walking along, tearing with his paws at the door and the window.

That didn't help me at all. He ignored 'no', even if I shouted it, which, at the end of an hour of this behaviour, I did. I stopped the car, when he barked, quite idiotically, at a field of sheep, got out, making sure we were on an isolated stretch of road, and shook him, which did my feelings more good than his.

By the end of three weeks he had stopped barking at cars behind us on the roads between towns, but he barked at everything and everyone when we went into towns. So I drove through all the island towns, until that too stopped.

By the end of March (the accident was in November) he was behaving more normally and drives weren't quite such a nightmare. Taking him out of the car was. He was terrified to shaking point of crossing busy roads. The car was now familiar, and again it was his sanctuary. And again he bolted for it whenever he was at any distance from it.

So back we went to car-parks and the 'in the car out of the car' game.

He had been sitting facing the car that crashed into us. He had seen it speeding towards him, heard it braking, seen the impact, heard the terrible explosive bang. I have never heard such a noise close to before. It was several weeks before I dared take him across the road, or walk him round the small towns.

I couldn't walk him in the lanes, as cars coming past us close sent him flying into the hedge, or into the ditch.

I had arranged, long before the accident, to go on Roy Hunter's American dog training course in April, and didn't want to miss it. The American methods are not quite like ours, and these courses had been well discussed and I very much wanted to know more about their ways with dogs.

I hadn't been on any drive longer than forty miles, because my neck hurt so much, and I hadn't driven on a motorway since the accident, apart from the one trip to Macclesfield for the PAT dog dinner. The course was at Writtle Agricultural College, near Chelmsford, and it was a very long way, especially with two dogs that were still nervous in the car.

It was possible to have one long drive, so I went over to Eric for the day for the first time for five months. Josse behaved on the motorway. There is little to see and no passers-by or wandering dogs, and he went to sleep. It took me some distance to get back my nerve. I watched every vehicle, expecting every single driver to do something daft, and was far more sensitive to other people's silly actions than I had been before. By the time I reached home that night I had recovered much of my nerve, though I still disliked anyone too close behind me and signalled them to overtake. I was constantly dropping back from cars in front as whenever I left what I felt was a reasonable gap, some idiot overtook me, and filled it. I felt safer with an empty road behind me.

The journey to Writtle became unexpectedly complicated.

I had written an article on dog training which had been published in the *Daily Telegraph* and had a surprising amount of correspondence from it, including a letter from Katie Boyle, who had photostatted it and was sending copies to people she felt needed educating on how to live with their dogs. She wanted to meet me.

I have never driven in London, and had no intention of doing so for the first time with a neck that wasn't yet working properly. Reversing was agony, and I had picked my route so that I was on familiar roads, as navigating alone is difficult, and I also wanted a route without too much motorway. I was breaking the journey by staying with friends *en route*. My friend Sheila and her German Shepherd Dog Coda were coming to Writtle too, which meant I would not be alone among people I had never met before.

Katie wanted me to meet John Fisher, who had invented the dog training-discs that had just come on to the market. I had been testing them as a training aid and found them excellent, especially for young puppies, as they were fascinated by the five brass discs that are held together by a piece of orange ribbon. I had met John at Trials, I realised when I saw him, but at that point had not associated the name and the face.

Finally it was arranged that I should drive South to meet John just off the M25, leave my car at his house, transfer myself and my dogs into his car, which has two dog cages, and he would drive me to Katie's. Katie lives near Hampstead. John lives near Guildford, so that proved more of an Odyssey than I had expected.

Also I had not met the M25. Having done so, I have no wish ever to meet it again. I drove with my heart in my mouth and my teeth gritted, and Josse barked his way down it, as we never had space behind us at all, and were in almost nose to tail traffic. It was no form of therapy after a road accident.

However, I made it, and met John and we reached Katie's. It was a vile day, with sleet in the air. Katie wanted to see my dogs, and we all piled into our cars, about six of us, as there were others there for me to meet, associated with dog rescue, and went off to Kenwood.

We had been travelling, almost non-stop, for three days. The dogs had slept with me in the hotel at Macclesfield, Josse now being able to come too, and provided he was put in the car with Chita when I went to eat, and could see me through the car window, parked outside the dining-room, he didn't yip. The next night we had stayed with a friend, where he settled quite well, but he had been very relieved to find he was coming in the car with me in the morning again. I suspected he might have felt he was going to be left behind when Chita and I departed.

He was quiet in John's car. He barked once or twice at traffic lights, when he saw a dog on the pavement, but for the most part travelled extremely well.

He was quiet on the way to Kenwood and so was Chita.

The weather had deteriorated, the woods being overhung with a pall of dark cloud, sulphur-tinged on the horizon. It was bitterly cold.

Dogs came out of all the cars for a walk on the common. There were other dogs everywhere, and I knew it would be more than Josse could take, especially as neither dog had had a proper run for three days. They needed to stretch their legs, but alone, unstressed. Even Chita was not yet easy when she went out and about, as there had been such a long period when both dogs stayed at home, and went nowhere except round the village, or played in our own grounds.

I took Josse out of the car, and he promptly went into a blind panic. John, used to problem dogs, took him from me, and found himself with a raving lunatic of a dog that had only one desire, to get to me or to get to the car. I was sure the dog was convinced he was being taken away from me by this man, and would never see me or Chita again. He was almost berserk.

John tried him on a Halti, which calms most dogs. The Halti was invented by Dr Roger Mugford, the animal behaviour consultant. It is very like a horse's head collar, fitting snugly over the dog's face and is ideal for those breeds which have thick fur and are being shown, as it means there is no neck chafing. It is also good for dogs that insist on pulling, which can damage their necks and throats. The dog is led by it, quite literally, by the nose, like a horse or a goat, and, once prejudice is overcome and people realise this is a training aid and not a muzzle, many owners find it easier than the slip chain. It had taught Anne Malcolm Bentzon's Samoyed, Sailor, not to pull, when everything else had failed. It didn't calm Josse. It made him worse, and after watching for a minute or so, I knew the

143

dog was working himself into a state of extreme stress and took him from John.

So John put Chita on her lead and took her out of his car. But Chita never goes with anyone else either. She did, after a fashion, walk with John.

Katie was astounded at the way the dogs behaved. I wasn't. Chita behaves for very few people indeed, yet with me she walks beautifully and never plays up. I still don't walk the two dogs in new places together as that turns into a competition. Chita is a front runner, and Josse wants to be well up with her. It's not worth the hassle of trying to keep them both from pulling me faster than I care to go.

Josse still stresses extremely fast, and neither dog could understand what was happening as both were in an entirely new situation. They were in a totally strange place, had been travelling in a strange car, and not even Chita had done that before, and now were being taken heaven knew where. They didn't know. I wondered if Chita could have caught Josse's fear that this was a preliminary to another abandonment on my part.

Within five minutes of reaching the common it began to snow heavily. Josse was lunging at passing dogs, Chita was pulling to get to me, and whatever we were having it wasn't a pleasant walk, so it was a relief to get back to the cars, and return to the warmth of Katie's lovely home and hot tea and biscuits.

We were all there because of our concern about abandoned dogs, about dogs' homes which are overcrowded and fuller by the day, and the numbers of dogs that are re-homed, often for no very good reason. Sometimes because the family have done all the wrong things, and turned the dog into an animal that they don't want and nobody else really does either. Both Katie's pedigree poodles came from Battersea Dogs Home, where they had been sent as unwanted, one of them with a major biting problem which is now completely cured. So many people buy a dog without thinking, or without researching the breeder, the breed, and the way the puppy was reared. Badly reared puppies turn into disastrous dogs.

That night I stayed with John and his wife and my dogs slept in his car in the garage. In the morning they were able to race in the fields, and work off some of the pent-up energy. We left for

Writtle on a Sunday afternoon, which proved to be the worst time I could have picked. I found myself hoping fervently the people who designed and built the M25 would spend their time in purgatory, where I was. At that point I was in stationary traffic at Hunton Bridge roundabout, where I spent about an hour, wondering what had happened to the village I knew where my husband's parents once lived, and where their old house was with relation to this modern nightmare.

It was a relief to reach Writtle and, after the evening meal, unload the dogs into the tiny cubicle they called a bedroom. There was just room to step between them when I got out of bed. I felt rather sorry for the students who have to live there for the duration of their course, but it was warm, and the food was magnificent.

I was on a fat-free diet, but the meals they produced for me were in many ways better than those that everyone else was eating.

The course was very professionally run and the American methods were not only fascinating but many of them have advantages over those we use in this country. I knew one or two of the other people, and found a number with whom I could talk.

Exercising the dogs was another matter as there were more than fifty people there and many had more than one dog. Many were not very sympathetic towards other people's problems, having easy dogs and being sure this was because they were well trained, rather than that they were very submissive, giving no problems.

I could exercise Chita among the others as she came when called, had no desire to spark at other dogs now, and kept beside me, at heel, rather than risk being rushed at by brash young fry. She did the equivalent of eyebrow raising at the youngsters with bad manners who ran or roared at her, and she gave me no problems whatever all week.

She did not like the area designated for communal use as a dog latrine, being fastidious in her ways, so we had to walk further than everyone else and find woods for her. Fortunately there was wild ground, woodland and a very pleasant walk away from traffic within half a mile. I took Josse to the same place, outside the grounds, so it was a very energetic week.

Josse was a very different matter to Chita, as he had now decided his duty was to protect my car from everyone. As the car-park was between the bedrooms and the lecture theatre, and the dogs were left there while I was in the dining-room or lecture theatre, every single person on the course and every single dog had to pass all the cars. Josse raged at them, especially when owners allowed their dogs to jump on the car, which was daily covered in muddy pawmarks as it was a very wet week with horible weather and high winds.

This didn't much please me as my car was very new and the paint was being scratched. I don't allow my dogs to jump at other people's cars, and if there is a dog inside a car we give it a wide berth. Few people on the course seemed to understand normal dog psychology. The American instructors did understand the problem.

By the time I took Josse out for exercise he had worked himself up into a royal state of rage, and no dog could come near us. I had to wait till everyone had gone in to eat and all dogs were out of the way for the first two days. I also had trouble in our corridor as though most people were considerate, two owners of very easy dogs let the dogs wander nonstop out of their open-room doors and Sheila and I finally had to operate an early warning system, with one of us standing guard to make sure the corridor was clear, as Coda was no more likely to tolerate a dog brushing past him in the narrow passage than Josse was.

Dogs are very territorial and this was common territory. A dog on its own, off-lead, was assuming a pack leader role and neither Josse nor Coda would have that. Chita didn't like it, but tolerated it, because by now she was well trained and under control although it was particularly hard for her as she is very much a pack leader in all situations if allowed to have her own way.

By the fourth day I was taking Josse out of the car when other dogs were about and he was behaving himself most of the time. A dog running by off-lead always triggered him to fury. But with the aid of a group of knowledgeable owners who kept their dogs on-lead and worked near me, I began to return him to what he had been before the accident.

He had also been quiet in the car once we were off the M25, so I had hopes that that too was cured.

I was wrong.

He learned at Writtle to bark at anyone near the car, and he barked continuously while travelling the day we left, almost without stopping, as everything that moved started him off. Sheila and I were breaking the journey to lunch with a mutual friend, and by the time we reached our destination, seventy miles away, I was exhausted.

I thought maybe the course had been a bad idea, as it hadn't helped Josse at all. Though he had settled to the odd routine, had behaved himself wonderfully at night, in spite of neighbours who came noisily up to bed at 2 am when we had been asleep for a couple of hours, their dogs sniffing under my door, and in spite of having eight dogs in a small space on the same floor.

The rooms being so small, the doors were very close together.

The course was probably a turning point.

He did become progressively easier to manage in the weeks that followed and by the time we had got to the date of the little show we were giving in aid of the guide dogs, to try and complete our third £1000, Josse was able to watch other dogs pass the car without barking, and come out with me, and behave perfectly, so long as I kept the exposure brief.

He slept most of the day of the show, which was very busy, as we had far more entries than we had expected and there were dogs galore everywhere. We had two disasters, as one of my club members parked her car near the little lake, on the bank, and while she was in the office, asking directions to the show field, her dog jumped on the handbrake and she came out to find the car settling nose down in eight inches of water.

That was the end of her day as it proved a problem for the RAC, and didn't come free till more than eight hours later, luckily with relatively little damage to car or dog. He was removed from it very early in the proceedings, though rather wetly.

The second incident was much more disturbing because a friend had with her her rescued Goldie, which had been abused as a youngster, and is still very difficult with some people and other dogs at times and which is now going blind. People around the car were upsetting him. My car and hers had been parked where we thought people would not go, but that is always a forlorn hope, and for some reason many children found it more convenient to go that way than the shorter way, and of course they wanted to talk to the dogs.

In the middle of the afternoon there was the most enormous crash. The Goldie had leaped at the driver's window, which was partly open to give him air, and had shattered it. The noise must have terrified him as he was cowering in the back of the car, the ground was littered with glass, the children had fled, and we never did find out what had actually happened.

His owner now has a cage for him. She had been sure he wouldn't take to it, but he behaves as if he has always travelled that way. The fact that Chita at the same age had taken to her cage without trouble did give his owner hope, which was justified.

I had had Josse exactly a year by the time we held the show. It was the anniversary of the day I brought him home.

Much of that year I felt defeated, especially after the crash which had cost me so dearly in his training and progress to a stress-free dog. Much of the time I felt we had made no progress whatever, and yet when I looked back, the progress was there. It comes slowly, almost invisibly, but it does come.

My life with him is made up of small highlights.

The twenty-mile drive which was only punctuated by three barks.

The first night he spent with me in the Macclesfield hotel and I was able to leave him and Chita, as I had always left her, and go to my evening meal, without a sound from him.

The day Liz came unexpectedly through the gate and he roared up to her, recognised her, and licked her hand.

His booster injection when he growled at the vet and instantly looked sheepish and offered him his paw.

148

The day he caught Chia, our Siamese, and terrified both Kenneth and me. She was in the flower-bed, and Josse sprang on her. He seemed to have his jaws round her. She screeched and fled, and Josse, called, came at once to me. I put him indoors and went in search of the cat, sure she had been injured.

I found her lying under a bank, soaking wet, for she had been well and truly licked. She appeared at first to be shocked but when I picked her up she began to purr and by the time she reached the house had quite recovered. There is never a tooth-mark on the birds he brings me, either.

Now we no longer need bother if he does go into Chia's part of the house. She doesn't like him, but she tolerates him, and he only noses her and comes away the second he is called.

The day we went to the Aquarium at Foel Ferry and the car parked three yards away had two Golden Retrievers beside it. I took Josse out of the car. He looked at them, and looked at me, and walked beside me, like a normal dog, though just once he looked as if he were about to bark.

No.

He trotted beside me, and I marked up another milestone.

People with normal dogs would never understand. Those with dogs that have been exposed, as Josse had, to one change after another, or with dogs that have suffered far worse than he, will know the sense of achievement.

This kind of training doesn't give titles or red prize cards, or certificates.

To the outsider it may seem insignificant, nothing.

To those who, like myself, have taken on a dog with problems, it will mean as much as it does to me.

Maybe Eric summed it all up in the piece he wrote for me, about Josse.

We may, just possibly, be able to compete in Obedience early next year, and maybe Trials will come, one day. I am going to try. But if he can't make it, if the stress is always too much for him, then that is the way it will be.

I will have done the best I know, but no way will I expose my dog to trauma for something that is a reward only for me. He would never know what those letters after his name meant, or what he had earned by his performance.

He may not make competition, but he will have had a life he enjoyed, and as I watch him run to the door and greet Liz, instead of barking at her continuously every time she appears, or lie, mouth open, laughing, as my baby grandson uses him as a mountain, I know that I now have a dog I can enjoy as a companion, and that he will, in his own way, reward me for deciding to take him into our home.

He is lying behind me now, sprawled out, totally at ease, and when I turn, his eyes meet mine and he stands and comes and leans against me and noses my hand, wanting, as always, that contact that is so much more important to him than it is to Chita.

Though he has taught her to want it too, and she has learnt a great deal from him.

The year has changed all three of us, and we have all learned a lot. Eric has learned too, as he doesn't usually have so much contact with a dog he has sold and Josse has made him think as much as he has made me think.

This is what he says.

Josse came to me in January 1985 from a colleague and fellow professional dog trainer. The dog had spent a couple of months at his boarding kennels, and had been partly trained in basic Obedience and looked very promising. His background is as Joyce describes it.

Chita was ageing and would soon be retired and Joyce had hinted that for her next dog a junior might be preferred rather than start over again with a puppy. She had seen some very nice junior dogs go through our training scheme and on to new homes.

I wondered if Josse would suit Joyce.

Josse had one hang-up in training and that was to run back to the kennel immediately he was asked to respond off the lead. So most of his training with me was achieved by patient off-lead praise-induced methods. This seemed to work with pleasing results. We all found him easy but he wasn't attached to any one person. He was shared between four people and accepted the situation.

Would he suit Joyce?

I thought so. I was sure so. I didn't, however, realise that with one person handling him all the time he would become so possessive and reluctant to be away from that person. Yes, we were to see a very different side to Josse in the months to come. He can certainly take advantage if the handler isn't quick enough.

[I am sixteen years older than Eric, which inevitably makes for slower reactions, and Eric is also unusually fast-moving and quick to respond when a dog plays up.]

If success is achieving the expected, and winning competitions then there are those who think she won't. If success is achieved by total commitment and the determination and enthusiasm that Joyce shows, then that is something else.

We wish Joyce every success with Josse.

It leaves me wondering just what success is. A dog to win prizes, or a dog that is a good companion and easy to take around?

I know which I prefer, and though I would like to try my hand with this one too at Trials, especially as Chita has reached retiring age, I won't grieve if we never make it. That isn't what dogs are about.

It's much easier to bring up a puppy than to take on a dog with a past, but the dog that has known other homes rewards you constantly, and Josse is proving the most affectionate dog I have ever owned, and, when not stressed by fear, is desperately anxious to please me.

It is an experience I wouldn't have missed for the world, and Josse, like my other dogs, teaches me daily.

Living with animals reminds me constantly of a friend of mine, Jim Gould, who provided material for two of my books and was one of the best farmers I have ever met. He said, 'I can tell you one way in which nature is always predictable. It is totally unpredictable!' He added that was why it was so fascinating as you never knew what would happen next, animals being animals.

So – where do we go from here?